T0283821

"Like so many other witches, my first witchc[...]
Scott Cunningham. I still use much of what I learned from him in my own books. He was a huge influence, personally and professionally irreplaceable and unmatched. It has always been a great sorrow to me that I never met Scott, but through this wonderful new biography, I feel as though I finally have. Thank you, Christine Cunningham Ashworth, for sharing him with me and the world. It is a gift beyond measure."

—Deborah Blake, author of *The Everyday Witch's Coven* and
The Eclectic Witch's Book of Shadows

"I loved this telling of Scott Cunningham's story! The format of including excerpts from other metaphysical writers was brilliant and lets us get to know Scott on the level he would have wanted us to—the spiritual one. Christine Cunningham Ashworth herself writes with such love and respect for her brother and their shared history. The combination makes a recounting of Scott's life that is as dreamy and whimsical as it is factual and informative. A must-read for those who found witchcraft through his books, whether that was decades ago or yesterday."

—Cassandra Snow, author of *Queering the Tarot* and *Queering Your Craft*

"Whether they realize it or not, all modern witches owe a great deal to Scott Cunningham. The fact that witchcraft is so accessible to curious seekers today is Scott's legacy. Written with such love and authenticity, *Scott Cunningham— The Path Taken* is a generous gift from Scott's own sister, Christine Cunningham Ashworth. This work offers us a rare opportunity to meet the man behind the books, and to properly celebrate Scott as a spiritual ancestor within the witchcraft community."

—Celeste Larsen, author of *Heal the Witch Wound*

"Applause and gratitude for the diligence, willingness, and courage of Christine Cunningham Ashworth to share so many personal stories and anecdotes of the Cunningham family. It is through her lens, her heart, her bravery that we can touch Scott Cunningham in a way many of us have only dreamed. Anyone blessed to own this book will have a true treasure in their hands. I know it will grow spiritual wings, fly to the furthest magical corners of the universe, and be a blessing to all who read its pages. A true keeper, a touchstone, a heartfelt working of love."

—Najah Lightfoot, author of *Good Juju* and *Powerful Juju*

"This book ought to come with a warning label: 'Do not open unless your schedule is free for the next several hours.' It's a hackneyed old trope to say, 'I couldn't put this book down,' but in the case of *Scott Cunningham—The Path Taken,* it's absolutely accurate. Christine's story is a truly compelling page-turner that reads like the best fiction, but even better, as it's all true! Whether you are a Scott Cunningham aficionado or are just getting introduced to his legacy in the world of witchcraft, you will be fascinated with this story of his courage, curiosity, and magic, written by one of the people who knew him the best—his sister. Just make sure you are ready to settle in for a nice, long, thoroughly enlightening, and enjoyable read."

—Madame Pamita, author of *Magical Tarot,*
Baba Yaga's Book of Witchcraft, and *The Book of Candle Magic*

"There are those who are legends from the early days of the modern Pagan movement. Many are well remembered, still beloved, their books still treasured. Scott Cunningham is such a legend, and this new biography is by someone who loved him, his sister, Christine Cunningham Ashworth. Beautifully written, *Scott Cunningham—The Path Taken* is a warm, funny, insightful portrait of a legend. Add this book to your shelf or book stack and meet the man you thought you knew. It's brilliant."

—H. Byron Ballard, author of *Seasons of a Magical Life*

"Christine Cunningham Ashworth's *Scott Cunningham—The Path Taken: Honoring the Life and Legacy of a Wiccan Trailblazer* gives us an invaluable peek into the Cunningham family dynamic. Christine lovingly shares details of her childhood growing up in Southern California during the '60s and '70s. A magical time. Station wagon-filled road trips and a family's love of adventure and the outdoors are the backdrop of pivotal moments that shaped their lives. Through memories and conversations, Christine grants us a private insight into the complexity of her older brother, Scott. The Universe whispered sacred secrets to Scott, and we all thank him and love him for sharing this wisdom with us."

—Steven Intermill, director, and Toni Rotonda, owner,
of the Buckland Museum of Witchcraft and Magick

"Ray and I were blessed to count Scott Cunningham as a good friend, and Chet Cunningham was inspirational in Ray's career. Christine absolutely brought Scott to life, and I laughed and cried along with her in this deeply personal biographical journey. This book offers wonderful insight into a life filled with light and love. Highly recommended!"

—Tara Buckland

"Christine Cunningham Ashworth has created a loving and insightful written journey to understand the many influences and experiences that shaped the man who would reshape Wicca—her brother Scott Cunningham. *Scott Cunningham—The Path Taken* is a beautiful book."

—deTraci Regula, author of *The Mysteries of Isis*

"As a biographer of individuals who have influenced our modern practice of magic, I've always yearned for a detailed look at their childhood and private lives. *Scott Cunningham—The Path Taken* will fill that need for generations to come. It is the true-life saga of a close-knit, loving family and the author's journey to piece together, from scattered memories, Scott Cunningham, the famous brother she never fully knew. It is about love and loss, regrets and appreciations—a memorial told in personal snapshot-like scenes, in the reminiscences of friends, and in the stories of people who only knew Scott Cunningham through his books that enriched and changed their lives.

"You will learn how Scott, writing in the 1970s and '80s, felt he had to live in two closets, both as a gay man and as a witch. Still, he legitimized solitary witchcraft by helping individuals 'remember' the natural, everyday practice of magic; he made Wicca, its knowledge, and essential practices, available to everyone. One takeaway from this book is to appreciate the people close to us—to pay attention to the things our loved ones do and say—and think about what you want to leave behind for those who come after."

—Mary K. Greer, author of *Women of the Golden Dawn*
and *Archetypal Tarot*

"In these pages, readers will find much more than a literary tribute to Scott Cunningham. Who was the person behind the pioneer? What was the power that illuminated his Pagan path? At once a biography and a work of spiritual scholarship, this book uses astrology, numerology, and magick to give us a holistic view of Scott Cunningham, not only as a dynamic practitioner but also as a deeply insightful soul. Because Scott laid the foundation upon which countless individuals have built their magickal practice, he is, in essence, every practitioner's spiritual sibling, and now his own sister, Christine Cunningham Ashworth, completes the circle by giving us an enlightening and beautiful book that does justice to his ongoing legacy. *Scott Cunningham—The Path Taken*, belongs on the shelf of anyone who is seeking—or has already found—a deeper connection to nature, magick, and our sacred selves."

—Antonio Pagliarulo, author of *The Evil Eye*

"A touching and intimate portrait of one of America's most important witchcraft pioneers, intensely readable and relatable, *Scott Cunningham—The Path Taken* is now required reading for anyone interested in Craft history. Thirty years after Cunningham's untimely passing, this book illustrates why his work is just as popular today as it was during his lifetime."

—Jason Mankey, author of *The Horned God of the Witches*

"Christine Cunningham Ashworth provides a detailed, respectful, and well-written biographical 'window' into the life story of the late Scott Cunningham—a prolific author of accessible, resourceful, and practical books on earth magic that are major knowledge resources and gateways for all who seek the ways of magic, especially solitary practitioners. If you have been touched by his work, you will treasure *Scott Cunningham—The Path Taken: Honoring the Life and Legacy of a Wiccan Trailblazer.*"

—Orion Foxwood, author of *The Flame in the Cauldron* and *The Tree of Enchantment*

Scott Cunningham

THE PATH TAKEN

Scott Cunningham

THE PATH TAKEN

HONORING THE LIFE AND LEGACY OF A WICCAN TRAILBLAZER

Christine Cunningham Ashworth

Foreword by Mat Auryn

WEISER BOOKS

This edition first published in 2023 by Weiser Books, an imprint of
Red Wheel/Weiser, LLC

With offices at:
65 Parker Street, Suite 7
Newburyport, MA 01950
www.redwheelweiser.com

ISBN: 978-1-57863-808-6

Library of Congress Cataloging-in-Publication Data available upon request.

Cover design by Sky Peck Design
Interior photos from the collection of Christine Cunningham Ashworth
Interior by Debby Dutton
Typeset in Adobe Garamond Pro, Orpheus Pro, and Proxima Nova

Printed in the United States of America
IBI

10 9 8 7 6 5 4 3 2 1

To everyone who found a home within the pages of Scott's books. This one is for you.

CONTENTS

EDITOR'S NOTE

Scott Cunningham (June 27, 1956–March 28, 1993) was a pivotal figure in the history of Wicca and witchcraft. A prolific author, even now—decades after his death—many of his books remain influential bestsellers. A comprehensive list of his publications may be found in Appendix I of this book.

It is impossible to overstate Scott's influence on the Western witchcraft world, as well as on Wiccan spirituality. His 1988 publication *Wicca: A Guide for the Solitary Practitioner* transformed the face of modern Wicca. Scott Cunningham did not introduce Wicca to the United States: that was Raymond Buckland. Nor is he the founder of modern Wicca: that's Gerald Gardner. Instead, Scott radically transformed this spiritual tradition and the way that it is practiced today. Scott Cunningham made Wicca and witchcraft accessible to all in a way that it had not been previously.

I recall when *Wicca: A Guide for the Solitary Practitioner* was first published and how controversial it was. Up until then, if you wanted to be a Wiccan, it was necessary to be initiated into an established lineage. Wicca was envisioned as exclusively coven-based: a group activity. This may not have been an issue for those residing in New York City or Chicago or some other big city, but for those living in other areas, especially rural regions, it could be prohibitive.

In those days before the internet, if you did not have access to an already established coven, it made initiation into Wicca extremely challenging, if not de facto impossible. Remember: this was during a time when openly admitting one was a witch or Wiccan was dangerous. Even now, as I write in 2022, there are places in the US where people feel safer wearing their pentacle jewelry hidden beneath their clothing. Imagine how it was in the 1980s.

In *Wicca: A Guide for the Solitary Practitioner*, Scott Cunningham wrote that one could initiate oneself into Wicca and taught us how. This was a revolutionary act of liberation that encouraged readers to claim their autonomy and take personal control of their own spiritual destinies. No need to relocate or to be dependent on the presence or compatibility of a coven. Scott publicly validated the path of the solitary practitioner. I cannot even begin to express how radical this was back in the '80s.

Scott's influence continues to impact the witchcraft world. His encyclopedias were, at that time, unique, especially *Cunningham's Encyclopedia of Magical Herbs* and *Cunningham's Encyclopedia of Crystal, Gem, and Metal Magic.* Until Scott, books in this vein were intended as academic reference: they rarely offered practical information. Instead, material was presented as superstition or folklore, a record of something archaic from the past. Scott's encyclopedias, on the other hand, were written by an unapologetic and knowledgeable modern practitioner for use by other modern practitioners. Every author of books containing practical information regarding witchcraft and especially encyclopedias devoted to it owes Scott a debt.

The transformations wrought by Scott Cunningham are so profound that he too often goes uncredited. Venture into any metaphysical shop today and you will most likely find a display of crystals for sale. Take it from me, that wasn't the case before the turn of the 21st century. In my opinion, their omnipresence is a direct result of Scott Cunningham's pioneering work on crystal magick.

Although the impact of Scott's work continues to grow, too many are unaware of Scott, himself. As you will read in these pages, he was a tremendously private person and so people tend to know the work, rather than the man. This brilliantly moving book written by Christine Cunningham Ashworth, Scott's younger sister, seeks to remedy that. Christine provides an intimate, personal, and unflinching look at Scott, herself, and their family. Although other books have been written about Scott, none have been so personal because no one else possesses this kind of knowledge. Christine generously shares her memories and family photographs, so that readers may gain insight into Scott's life and feel that we "know" him.

What is remembered lives.

Judika Illes

FOREWORD

Scott Cunningham remains the pinnacle and gold standard of success when it comes to witchcraft books. Even today, three decades after he left this world, many of his books remain bestsellers within our genre. "You're the new Scott Cunningham" is a phrase that I have heard more times than I can count since I published my first witchcraft book. I'm not alone in this. This is something that's been said to virtually any cisgender male witchcraft author, especially if they're queer, whose books do well, including my husband Devin Hunter when he wrote his first book. Scott remains the definitive standard by which to compare success in the niche field of occult writing.

Here's the thing, though: there was only one Scott Cunningham, and there will only ever be one Scott Cunningham. It's not even about how wildly successful his books are; it's about the impact he had on seekers and practitioners of witchcraft and Wicca, as well as on the public perception of these paths during the height of an era in the United States deemed "the Satanic Panic." During this era in the 1980s, anything even slightly metaphysical or anything that strayed from the Christian Church was demonized and slandered in a paranoid frenzy fueled by the media—to the point of people losing their jobs, their homes, their kids, or in cases such as that of Damien Echols and the

West Memphis Three, losing their freedom and ending up on Death Row under false charges.

Through his books, writings, videos, and media appearances, Scott helped to demystify the practices and beliefs of the witch that were once shrouded in mystery and fear. Scott wrote at a time when very few publicly accessible book resources existed—a time before the internet. He shared information that most would otherwise need to seek out a coven for training and initiation to learn. Scott presented a radical idea through his works, that the practice of witchcraft was one that anyone could embark on and that it was as much a spirituality as it was a religion. What I mean by "spirituality" is that Scott strongly advocated through his writings that witchcraft could be a personal solitary practice that nourished the soul and strengthened one's connection with Nature, divinity, and life itself. For Scott, it didn't matter whether or not you were initiated into a tradition or practicing with a coven. Scott's work was firm that anyone who desired could learn and engage in the ways of the witch.

Today, that may not seem like anything revolutionary, and that's mostly because of the work that he and his peers, including Silver Raven Wolf and Raymond Buckland among others, did, leading to the present accessibility of witchcraft information. At the time, writing that witchcraft—and specifically Wicca—could be a solitary path was revolutionary and controversial within the witchcraft community. Just as progressive and important was Scott's inclusivity in his writings and work. Witchcraft was for *everyone*, regardless of sex, gender, ethnicity, age, or disabilities. Scott understood that everyone has access to magick; all we must do is choose to connect with it and embrace it.

Scott's monumental impact and legacy is his own, and no one could ever take that away or fill those shoes. His True Will (a concept within occultism meaning one's life's purpose and work) was his own. The work he did is something that no one can ever go back and do themselves at the crucial moment in history when he did it. The work that I and many others do today would not be possible without pioneering writers like Scott.

Unfortunately, I never got the chance to meet Scott. He passed away around the time that I was just beginning to explore the writings of witchcraft myself as a child, including his books. Despite this, in many ways, I feel like I know Scott. On one level I know him through his writings, as all his readers do. But as an author myself, I also know that you never truly know someone from their books alone. I consider Scott Cunningham an ancestor of mine. I don't mean that we're blood related. In witchcraft there are other types of ancestors that we honor, including those who are ancestors of the path of witchcraft itself and ancestors of the vocational work we do in the world, such as writing witchcraft books.

I've worked closely with Scott as an ancestor, and have received much guidance, assistance, synchronicity, and appearances in my dreams from him. In fact, I strongly believe that Scott led me to Christine Cunningham Ashworth, and I'm sure she would agree. I am not even sure how Christine and I first crossed paths or started talking; I didn't even realize that she was Scott's sister initially. Once I did, I eventually and with some reluctance told her about my ancestral work with Scott and the dreams in which he appeared. She confirmed that everything sounded just like Scott and that she was certain that he was visiting me, as he does for so many others.

The first time I met Christine in person was a couple of years later at The International Divination Event in Texas. Christine was grounded, warm, loving, and welcoming. Despite meeting her for the first time, I felt like I had known her for years and was already part of her family. That's the same energy that she imparts within this book, welcoming you into the Cunningham family, sharing not only memories and stories, but also family history.

While reading this book, I gained new perspectives and insights on Scott's own writings. For example, Scott famously and controversially writes in his *The Complete Book of Incense, Oils, and Brews* that "Rosemary can be safely used for any other herb." This is something that has puzzled a lot of witches, including myself. However, reading about the special relationship that Scott had with rosemary made it all make sense. It becomes pretty clear throughout this book that rosemary was a dear plant spirit ally of his, so of course with that strong spiritual connection he had with rosemary, it would be willing to assist him in ways that the magickal properties of the plant itself didn't naturally lend itself to others. It also made me realize that when Scott is giving an example in his writing of how to work with a plant, his go-to herb was often rosemary. Christine Cunningham Ashworth's book provides many other glimpses of insight into his writing, helping one to get a clearer picture of the whys and hows of his books by learning about who he was as a person.

As flattering as it is, maybe it's not so much that I'm the new Scott Cunningham or that someone else is. At least, not in the sense that people will say, for example, "Lady Gaga is the new Madonna." Rather, perhaps we are in alignment with the spirit of Scott Cunningham in the sense of continuing his legacy. Because Scott's legacy had nothing to do with book sales; nor is it about any one individual. His legacy is about witchcraft itself. That includes all who have read Scott's work, have taken on the mantle of the word "witch" or "Wiccan" as a personal path of spirituality, who contribute to that path through writing, teaching, creating community, and embracing inclusivity within it. It's all a continuation and descendant of the legacy and memory of Scott's work and impact, just as his work was the continuation of the legacy of and the descendant of those witchcraft influences before him. Scott's legacy lives on through its monumental impact he had upon witchcraft, how it's spoken about, written about, taught, and practiced. The spirit of his legacy lives on through all of us who were influenced by his works knowingly or unknowingly, which is why his books remain just as important and relevant to us today and will be for quite some time.

In witchcraft, we have a saying when it comes to those who have crossed the veil: "What is remembered lives." In the Craft, it's important that we remember those who came before us, especially those who helped to open the way in a major way. Scott is definitely remembered, and will be for a very, very long time. Here within the pages of this book, we have a collection of intimate memories of Scott Cunningham being preserved from a perspective that no one else could ever provide, the memories of the woman who grew up with him as her older brother. Through these memories, Scott lives on more than ever. As I read this book, I laughed at times and I teared up during others, as Christine lovingly and honestly shares Scott's story. But most of all, I found that I couldn't put it down—it was such a great read. Here, through these memories, Scott is more alive than ever since his passing. He's not just remembered in this book as this prolific Wiccan author. Here he's remembered, honored, and loved as Scott, the person, the brother, the son, the friend, as well as the witchcraft writer.

—Mat Auryn, author of *Psychic Witch* and *Mastering Magick*

PREFACE

Why did I write this book? Let me give you some perspective; my dad, Chet Cunningham (1928– 2017), received his master's degree in journalism in the early 1950s from Columbia University in New York. He wrote daily—magazine columns, training films, whatever paid, plus novels on his down time. I vividly remember falling asleep to the sound of his manual typewriter. Through dogged determination and an unwillingness to ever give up, Chet had over three hundred and fifty novels published during his lifetime, plus over sixty non-fiction novels.

My brother, Scott Cunningham, was born on June 27, 1956, and passed away on March 28, 1993. He was also a writer, one who specialized in metaphysical non-fiction books that set the Wiccan world alight. Through his writings, he gave not only permission, but the tools, to anyone who wished to follow a Wiccan path without having access to a coven. His books were practical and informative, his tone one of openness and kindness. The books were easy to understand and had extensive bibliographies, which encouraged others to seek out more knowledge from the very sources he had used. See Appendix I for a list of his writings.

As more than one voice in this book will tell you, this idea of not having to be in a coven was both energizing and polarizing. He (along with a few of his peers) helped to change the face of witchcraft, and

Wicca, forever. His life, so short, meant that while his books reached a wide audience, people never got the chance to know him, the reserved man behind the widely read books.

Me? My name is Christine Cunningham Ashworth, and I'm Scott's younger sister. From 1973 to his death in 1993, we were close, though Scott was a deeply private person. I have been writing since 2000; my first novel was published in 2011. I have over ten novels published and multiple short stories and novellas, along with one other non-fiction book that I published in 2019. My own writing journey didn't really start until after Scott had died.

My brother Greg is also published in fiction under a pseudonym. My mom told us bedtime stories. We were also voracious readers. All three of us kids were immersed in words from our very beginnings.

And so the book begins . . .

If I had known my older brother Scott would be so beloved, so polarizing, so prolific, and would die so young, I, in my youth, would have taken notes. Kept all our correspondence. Taken more photos. Or perhaps had a cassette deck tape recorder going whenever we talked.

But I didn't. So here we are.

Memories are, at best, crystal-clear images frozen in time. Sound, scent, sight, taste, touch, all right there, so vivid. At their worst, memories are foggy, amorphous, intangible things that no one can verify. A pity that all I have is my memories . . . but both my parents are gone, so it's up to me now. Throughout this book I have added snippets of conversations. Most of them took place in one form or another. They are not word-by-word conversations. What they are is what memory has given me, whether through family repetition (stories told again and again), or what might have been said in a private setting that rings true.

The longer I work on this labor of love, the more snippets come to me. Bits of conversation. Colors. The heat of the day, or the cool of an air-conditioned hotel room, the scent of a city. I'm trusting these snippets and sharing them with you.

I am not an historian. I don't have dates of his major life events written down. I don't have salacious details of his deeply personal life (and even if I did, I wouldn't share them). I have not memorized every one of Scott's books. Hell, I didn't even read most of them until after he died.

That's a confession, by the way.

What I am is the younger sister who alternately adored him and ignored him; and he did the same with me.

This is where I need to tell you that, in reading those books he wrote, I saw a side of him I never saw in person, heard a voice I had never heard from him before. It both pleases me and saddens me. Pleases, because now all I need to do is pick up his books and he is there with me. Saddens, because I never got to see that part of him in real life.

So it goes.

It has struck me now that once I let this book out into the world, my memories won't be my own anymore. They will be seen by you. Known by you. Filtered through your experience. My words, yes, but your internal translation.

A part of me is hesitant, now that I near the end of this journey.

I have to laugh . . . when I wrote that, I swear I heard Scott sigh and tell me to get on with it, already. So here I go . . . getting on with it.

From my heart to yours.

AUTHOR'S NOTE

In talking with friends about this book while it was in progress, one mentioned that it would be wonderful to read about Scott's astrology chart. Another mentioned numerology. And from there, the idea blossomed, as in my own practice, I am learning astrology and numerology and the tarot.

I reached out to friends to ask if they would help me out. Some I asked for their expertise; others I asked because of our long friendship. Some gave me stories; some put context to Scott's work; some gave me definitive details of signs and numbers and tarot spreads, and how they relate to Scott's life here. I am blessed to have such friends.

I hope these words give you more insight to the person Scott was, and the impact he had on our world.

AND ANOTHER THING . . .

A year or so after Scott died, our dad, Chet Cunningham, urged Llewellyn Worldwide, Scott's publisher, to take the autobiography that Scott had started and turn it over to friends of his to complete, using the materials Scott had left behind. David Harrington and deTraci Regula agreed to take on the task, but Dad had a stipulation.

Christine and Scott, 1961.

Apparently, Dad wanted to make sure there was no mention of Scott's sexuality in the book. He didn't see any reason at that time to let people know how he died. To Chet Cunningham, AIDS carried a stigma that he did not want attached to his son. From what I understand, Llewellyn agreed to that stipulation and as far as I know, continues to carry out Chet's wishes on this matter. I do not fault them for it at all.

Now it's three decades later. The governmental response to the AIDS epidemic still infuriates me. There is nothing shameful about being gay, or bisexual, or a lesbian, or asexual, or transgender, or any other way of being that isn't straight, cisgender heterosexual. We're all human. Love is love is love in all its many and varied forms and should always be celebrated. There can never be too much love in the world.

Scott had no time for haters of any stripe. He would have loved all the queer magick books that have been published in the past decades.

He would have loved knowing that perhaps he helped a marginalized youngster find their way in the world through his writings on magick. And while he would have understood our dad's position at the time, he would also be absolutely fine with me bringing it into the light in this day and age.

I'm not about to set aside or ignore that important aspect of Scott's life. But neither do I go into great detail about his love life because I don't have those details. Even if I did, I wouldn't share them. Scott was a deeply private person and I respect that. I also believe, were he alive today, he'd be an activist in the LGBTQIA+ community.

Love is love is love.

Always.

ACKNOWLEDGMENTS

My thanks first and foremost must go to Arwen Lynch Poe, who talked me into sharing a room with her at the Northwest Tarot Symposium in Portland, Oregon, in March of 2018, thus re-starting my own metaphysical journey.

From there, my thanks go to Dru Castle, Trisha Parker, and all the people at Phoenix Phyre, a Pagan gathering in Florida, who had me come to speak about Scott in October of 2018. When I had finished, so many people came up to tell me I must write a book about my brother. Thank you, thank you, thank you. Along the same vein, many thanks to the Trees of Avalon Pagan Gathering in the Ocala National Forest, for having me in 2019 and 2022. Tina Miller Jesko, your belief in me and your friendship, the grace and kindness of everyone I met there, is a bright spot in my life.

Amber Highland and Jaymi Elford, for being there since the very beginning with love, support, and a listening ear. Beverly Frable, who added the spark that helped this book bloom. My brother Greg Cunningham, who read so many iterations of this book and offered me his own memories. My love and gratitude to you all are immense.

To Mat Auryn, who, when I was struggling with this book, offered to write the foreword for me. Mat, we barely knew each other, and your first book hadn't even come out yet; but your belief in me, and your innate kindness, gave me strength when the writing became difficult. My deepest gratitude and love.

To Stephanie Rose Bird, Amy Blackthorn, Ethony Dawn, James Divine, Jaymi Elford, Amie Emberharte, Storm Faerywolf, Beverly Frable, Nancy Hendrickson, Dorothy Morrison, Nicholas Pearson, Lynne Redd, Michelle Welch, and Benebell Wen, heartfelt hugs and love to you for being willing to contribute to this labor of love.

Most of all, to my husband, Thomas W. Ashworth (look up his IMDB), who watched me fly to writing conferences, Pagan gatherings, and metaphysical conferences, and who always welcomed me home with so much love. You make this life so much *more*. Your creativity, spark of divine madness, tenacity, and dedication to your Craft always, always push me to be at my best. And when I can't be, you're there to help me rest. Love of my life, my partner, my friend. Thank you.

Last but never least, to my dear editor, Judika Illes, and the entire Weiser team, my profound thanks and gratitude and love.

CHAPTER ONE

Hearts, Stars, and Numbers

LOSING SCOTT

In March 1990, I had received a phone call from our dad, author Chet Cunningham, telling me that Scott was in the hospital in Massachusetts, and he was very ill.

I knew that Scott was on a book tour on the East Coast, put together by his publisher. He had a couple of people with him to handle details, staffers for the publisher I presume. At any rate, they did quite a bit of travel, starting in Boston and going from there. The following is what I have been told by Dad.

In Salem, the staffers came to pick Scott up from his hotel, but he wasn't waiting in the lobby as usual. Concerned, they called up to his room, but there was no answer. After talking to the hotel manager, he finally agreed to go up and open the room for them, in case something was wrong.

They found Scott on the bed, dressed but semi-conscious. Somehow, they roused him, packed his bags, and they all bundled into a taxi and got him to the best hospital in Massachusetts—Mass General, back in Boston. This was about an hour's drive, from what I understand.

Scott was admitted immediately. A day or so later, and after several tests were done, he was diagnosed with cryptococcal meningitis, a type of fungal disease that is impossibly rare, but that he developed due to his already-compromised immune system.

In short, he had AIDS.

I wanted to go to Scott, to be his advocate. Both Dad and my husband, Tom Ashworth, refused to let me, as I was three months' pregnant with our first child and a hospital was no place for a healthy pregnant woman. Instead, Dad went. When it became obvious that Scott wouldn't be strong enough to travel for quite a while, Dad ended up coming home and Scott stayed for several weeks before he was able to fly back to California. Once back in San Diego, he was immediately transferred to UC San Diego Medical Center, the same hospital where he had conquered his cancer in 1983.

I didn't see Scott for months, until he was back on his feet; and by the time I did, I was very pregnant, and he looked almost normal, if a bit on the thin side. He was sick, yes, but he didn't *look* sick; rather, it looked like he had beaten it back. He was on daily medications, but I have no knowledge of which medications.

Since AIDS had been around for a decade at this point, I figured he would beat it with the new drugs available. The fact that he was still alive was a strong argument, to me, that he'd do just fine. After all, in 1983 alone, between my husband and me, we lost over fifty people we knew in the theater world to AIDS, and in a very short timeframe—less than six months. The shock as they fell, one by one, seemingly out of the blue, had stunned us. We had watched and raged when the government was slow to react. I hated the homophobia, the closed-mindedness, the smugness of cis-het people as gay men died by the thousands and thousands worldwide. But ten years on, I clung to the fact that medical advances surely had come far. Surely, he'd recover, even though it seemed AIDS was still pretty much a death sentence.

Whatever medications Scott was prescribed in the beginning, it was just before they had come up with the cocktails, those mixes of medicines that were promising. By the time they had worked out the formulas and started prescribing those cocktails, Scott was no longer a candidate to take them. The disease had progressed too far.

Once Scott and I had moved out of the family home in 1978, Dad had taken down the wall between his den and the boys' room and made it one big den slash office. He put a small couch in there, and Mom had her desk too, though she didn't spend much time there anymore. She'd long stopped being able to proofread for Dad. When Scott came home from UCSD Medical, they put him in my old bedroom on a temporary basis until he was well enough to go back to his own apartment, which he did about a month later. Luckily, he'd moved from his apartment on Orange Avenue the previous year, and his new place wasn't far from the parents.

After the AIDS diagnosis in 1990, a lot of my memories are fuzzy, and I'm blaming that on being pregnant and then the new baby (or let's just call the little darlings "sleep deprivation experiments," shall we?). Tom and I would come down to San Diego for holidays, birthdays, Mother's Day and Father's Day, as well as a random weekend here and there, and we'd see Scott. I remember my oldest brother Greg was dating someone new, having gotten a divorce a year or so earlier. Scott most emphatically did not like Greg's new significant other (Scott called her the Sergeant) and did not think she was a good match for Greg, though I don't know if he ever told Greg that.

Dad and I kept in loose, but fairly regular, contact. Our family, well. If there's one thing we're not good at, it's reaching out and calling each other (this was pre-cell phones, people). But I knew pretty much how Scott was doing. I knew he was still writing, and still teaching to some extent. Scott and I would mail each other cards, just because. Mine to him still usually had a check in it, though I thought it was totally unnecessary at that point. Why? Well . . .

The answer goes back to 1979 and the early 1980s, after I moved up to Los Angeles to be with my husband Tom (we married in February of 1980). Every now and then, once I had a fairly regular job or at least a temp job from one of the temp agencies I was with, I would send Scott a check and a card, kind of out of the blue. At least, to me it was out of the blue. He would send me cards and letters now and then. We kept that correspondence up until he got too sick and moved in with my parents in late 1992, even though his book sales in the later years were, I assumed, keeping him mostly comfortable.

◊◊◊

In 1992, not sure which month but early, probably January, I had come down to see the parents, since it had been a while. Scott and I went to a late lunch together, as it had been . . . well. This was most likely the first time we'd ever gone out to eat together in years that didn't involve fast food.

I told him I was making the trip from L.A., and I'd love to take him to lunch at his favorite restaurant. After all, I had the fancy job at Candle Corporation, a privately held mainframe computer software company, and I could afford it.

We went to a place in Hillcrest, and I drove. He still looked like the brother I grew up with, but his vision was dicey at this point. Not gone, but he had difficulty with depth perception, and hadn't driven a car in quite a while.

We got out of the car and he just stood there, sunglasses covering his eyes. Finally, he sighed.

"I'll need your help. I can't see the ground very well. How far are we to the restaurant?"

"Not far." I slid my arm around his waist. His arm went around my shoulder. "We have about twenty paces until there are steps."

We walked until just before the stairway. "Okay, wait. Now reach forward with your left hand, there's a railing there. Feel it? Good. Scoot a foot forward until you feel the cement. Now step up. And another step. One more. Can you see the door?"

"Yeah." He squeezed my shoulder and opened the door.

Oh, how I wish now I had a tape recorder that could have recorded the conversation. Our topics were wide-ranging.

During our lunch, he spilled the beans about those checks I used to send him. He confessed to me that in the early '80s, when he was desperate for grocery money, or money to keep the lights on, he'd do a money spell. And most of the time? I answered that spell with a quick note or card, and a check for $25 or $50, depending on what kind of job I had at the time. I just laughed when he finally told me, because that was so quintessentially Scott. And likewise, it was so very much "me" to respond to his unspoken need, sent out to the Universe. We were linked not only by love, but by our sibling bond.

I know to my soul he told me secrets and he told me truths and he told me that life doesn't stop at death, and to not be sad for him. That was the first time he mentioned death to me, as in *his* death.

He also told me how he was fighting this thing inside him. Fighting it with visualization and magick, and with the help of the Goddess and the God. That's how he got rid of the non-Hodgkin's lymphoma a decade or so earlier. He said he had too much still to do with this life, that he wasn't ready. He had more books to write, more people to reach, and he was running out of time.

Because I hadn't read his books, I didn't entirely understand the pain in his voice when he mentioned the books he still needed to write, and how he felt he was letting people down, but he just couldn't write fast enough. I said that the main thing that made me sad was that he never found the love of his life. He shrugged. He told me he'd tried, but love wasn't for him, and he'd made his peace with it. He also told me he'd been celibate for more than a decade. He figured the virus that was killing him had been inside him for years at that point.

Our conversation was at times filled with urgency, and at times calm, desultory. I spilled secrets I hadn't shared with anyone, and he didn't judge me. I drank wine. He did not. We were there for at least two hours. We laughed, and I cried, and we ate and drank and behaved, finally, like grown-ups. I was thirty-one, he was thirty-five.

We had roughly a year left to share this plane of existence.

The Natal Chart of Scott Cunningham

By Benebell Wen

Let's begin with Mr. Cunningham's sun, moon, and rising, which are Cancer under the decan ruler Venus, Aquarius under the decan ruler the Moon, and Leo rising under the decan ruler Mars, respectively. I'm working with Tropical Whole Signs but will from time to time reconcile with Cunningham's sidereal chart.

Here we see someone who will present as introverted and pensive, but who is prone to eccentric ideas and fiercely independent-willed in the life path he will choose for himself. Venus in the eleventh also means he likes to keep eccentric friends. Those in his social circle will be just as artistic and independent-minded as he is. Cunningham, and the company he keeps, will diverge from the mainstream.

With his ascendant flanked on either side by Pluto and Jupiter, he won't have an easy life, and will likely have been tailed by spirits from beyond the veil since childhood (Pluto's effects), yet as we can now affirm in retrospect, one whose legacy will certainly be remembered, and whose influence will continue far beyond his lifetime (Jupiter's effects on the ascendant).

With Leo rising, his innate mission in life is to manifest creativity in his work products, and to attain recognition for his creative work. If the Path he wants to walk has not already been paved by another, he will pave it himself. That's the Leo rising charge in him.

Physically, he would have soft, pleasing features and doe eyes, which are typical of Cancer suns. He also would have been more

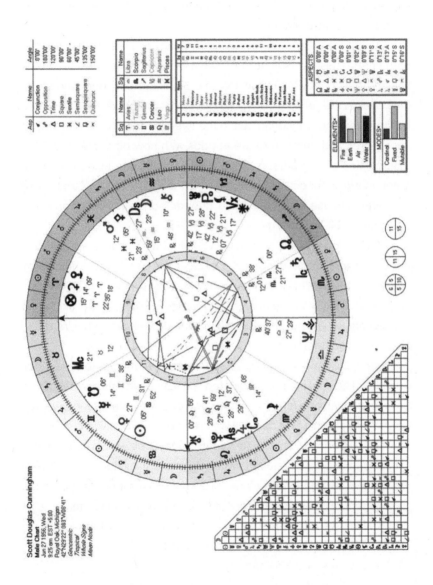

sensitive than he'll let on—taking criticisms too personally, overthinking what people say to him, though on the magnanimous side, deeply empathetic toward others.

Cunningham is air-dominant and fixed-dominant with a diurnal birth chart. Thus, he was born to be seen, though, with his sun in the twelfth house (under a Tropical Whole Signs system), one who struggles against the persona, or social mask, that the public has pressured him to wear. The Cancerian sun in the twelfth can indicate one whose internal self and true nature are at odds with how others perceive the externalities of that person. Twelfth house suns can also indicate an emotional disconnect with the biological father. They say that those with twelfth house suns fight many inner demons and are most fixated on spiritual self-knowledge.

Part of the air dominance in Mr. Cunningham's chart is attributed to the Grand Trine connecting the air signs in the air houses. That means he is likely to excel in writing, research, and discernment. Plus, his Mercury in Gemini is a strong placement for high intellect, verbal skills, and a penchant for writing. As if to amplify that, he was born on a Wednesday, the Day of Mercury.

With his Chiron in Aquarius, we see one who tends to be a loner, or outlier. The soul imprint associated with Chiron in Aries is that of The Savant, one who is a learned scholar and one who seeks to know. Cunningham is a born philosopher. If we are to get into past life contemplations, the seventh house Chiron might suggest one who had difficulties in marriage or difficult relations with government institutions in his past life, and with a moon in Aquarius, one who was male presenting in the most recent past incarnation, and one who was a religious man.

In terms of divine resonances, according to his birth chart, he would be closely attuned to a maternal goddess of the hearth, a Vesta, Hestia, or Ceres goddess archetype.

His early childhood was likely unconventional, with an unconventional mother, given the Aquarius moon. Plus, an Aquarius moon shows one who is eccentric, avant-garde, mystical, and will take the road less traveled to achieve his life purpose. And he probably gets that from his mother. The Aquarian moon can also indicate one who yearns to openly practice and teach that unconventional perspective of mysticism. Aquarian moons tend to become teachers, revolutionary leaders, and seek emotional fulfillment through achieving a greater good.

Some birth charts indicate greater career success if one stays close to home while others indicate greater opportunities for success if one leaves home and goes far away. In Cunningham's chart, if he leaves home and traverses afar in his twenties, he'll meet opportunities that take him toward greater professional success.

The Taurus midheaven and Virgo in the second house tie his professional interests closely to the land, and specifically to flora and the plant kingdom. Although we now know factually the career trajectory he took, assessing the Taurus midheaven under a Saturn decanate ruler with Saturn in the oppositional fourth house, Cunningham would have had a promising career in a traditional corporate setting, and I would even go so far as to say he would have succeeded in executive leadership. It's that retrograde Saturn under Scorpio pulling in opposition to his midheaven that will create deeply divided forking paths throughout his life, forcing him to choose between oppositions.

Let's talk about the Sagittarius north node, or some of the generalities attributed with that. Often the story told here is someone from a small town who ventures into the big city, someone from humble roots with grandiose dreams of adventure and exploration. Plus, with his Lot of Fortune in House Nine, the house most influenced by Sagittarius, he'll find his fortunes far from home. His impact will travel far beyond his local roots.

Revisiting what we said earlier about one who prefers a solitary life, those with a Lot of Fortune in Aries tend to prefer standing alone and standing part. They'll find their own way through life and won't do well if they get micro-managed. The corporate life might not be for them, no matter how potentially great they would be in that arena.

For those open to the concept of reincarnation and past lives, Mars in the eighth house can indicate someone who lived through a war in a past life, and thus in the present life, experience certain forms of subconscious inherited trauma that will govern behavior and thought process. Aquarian moon in the seventh conjunct with his descendant, per past life astrology, is interpreted as one who was a man in the past life incarnation that has the most impact on the karma of his present life as Scott Cunningham, and this man that he was would have been handsome, serious-looking, still just as eccentric as Cunningham is, and one who strayed from social norms—perhaps a revolutionary leader to some capacity. Pisces in the eighth can also indicate a man who, in this past life, experienced a cataclysmic loss in wealth, estates, assets, or social standing (thus compelling him to join a revolution?), and the karmic aftereffects of that are likely to percolate into the present life of Scott Cunningham.

Also, in terms of ancestral lineage, an innate, instinctual predisposition toward witchcraft runs in the family—it's in his blood.

The eighth house in our chart is the resident house of crisis and transformation, so Mars here can mean that Cunningham will undergo major personal transformations through each milestone of his life path.

This is not someone who remains static. Who he becomes as an adolescent will be diametrically different from his persona as a child, and who he becomes in his twenties will be diametrically different from his adolescent persona. In his thirties, yet again, he'll transform dramatically, and so on.

With Mars ruling and empowered in the eighth house, and under watery, spiritual Pisces, the placement of Mars will have a greater influence over Cunningham's life trajectory. An eighth house Mars further underscores the earlier implications of one who fights inner demons. This Mars placement is a sign of one who possesses incredible potential for metaphysical development and one who wields a strong power of attraction, a power he can learn to wield, control, and use to his personal advantage.

But the dark side to that power is one who is at a greater risk of destroying himself with all the intensity he exudes. Someone with such a Mars placement will need to learn how to quickly and expediently calm his emotions, practice grounding meditation, and take extra efforts to shield himself from others' emotional manipulation. Otherwise, these psychic effects can lead to psychosomatic symptoms and physical health complications.

The sixth house in our charts reveals matters pertaining to physical health. Retrograde Hygeia and black moon Lilith here under Capricorn in his sixth suggest battles with health complications throughout his life, especially when it comes to his blood vessels, blood, bones and his skeletal system, or the excretory system.

There are a lot of personal sensitive points applying pressure in Cunningham's sixth house, which in traditional medical astrology, is said to weaken one's immune system and cause one to be more susceptible to external infections, invasions of bacteria or viruses, etc. (The

Scott, 1987.

direct interdependence between the skeletal system and immune system are now well-documented, so here, we are likely to see health complications originating from bone marrow.) Lacking elemental Earth in his chart, his physical constitution is more prone to being calcium and protein deficient, so those are nutrients for him to be ever mindful of.

NOTES: This natal chart reading is based on the birth details provided by Christine Cunningham Ashworth, cast as Tropical Whole Signs and set with a Mean Node.

Scott by the Numbers

By Nancy Hendrickson

Numerology—often relegated to the divination corner—is an accurate method for predicting many facets of a person's life, much like the information gained from an astrological chart. The method of numerological calculation itself is simple. By using an alpha-numeric format, an individual's name and birthdate can be parsed in several ways, giving us the primary numbers for life path and destiny as well as secondary numbers showing challenges, karmic influences, and life pinnacles.

The format for calculation is to substitute numbers for letters.

a, j, s	b, k, t	c, l, u	d, m, v	e, n, w	f, o, x	g, p, y	h, q, z	i, r
1	2	3	4	5	6	7	8	9

When adding together numbers for name or birthdate, the sum is always reduced to nine or less, *with the exception of eleven, twenty-two, and thirty-three*, which are Master Numbers. There will typically be multiple reductions until nine or less is reached. For example: February 14, 1990, calculates to: 2 (February) + 5 (1+4) + 1990 (19/10/1) = 2 + 5 + 1 = 8

The most important numbers in numerology are:

Birthdate (Life Path)
Expression (Destiny)
Vowels in the birth name (Heart's Desire)
Consonants (Personality)

Calculations can also be done showing how an individual operates on each plane of expression (physical, mental, emotional, intuitive), as well as any hidden challenges or karmic lessons. Using the birthdate, timing events can be calculated for the year, month, and day.

Scott's Numerological Overview

Scott Douglas Cunningham was born on June 27, 1956. The numbers associated with his full name at birth as well as his birthdate tell us many things about his all-too-short life. Scott was idealistic, open-minded, and a humanitarian. However, his compassionate nature would often put him at odds with his results and goal-driven personality. Success would have been easier for him than for most; however he would have had difficulty balancing physical success with his psychic and intuitive sensitivities.

Scott was born to leadership. He was a self-starter and fascinated by how to design systems that were both practical and yet fit into his magickal worldview. Scott was intuitive, a born idealist, forgiving, opti-mistic and supportive of others. He was a diplomat with patience for others' struggles, but his empathetic nature could wage war with the part of him that wanted to place himself in a bubble in order to work. Scott was sensitive to the world around him, which would, again, have made it imperative to balance on the thin edge between the world of spirit and the world of the physical.

Scott was entrepreneurial and dedicated. Given his numbers, had he lived, I believe he would have become an eco-warrior, taking on climate change as a major magickal focus.

Scott's Life Path

Scott's Life Path—calculated by his date of birth—is the number nine. Nine is the number of the humanitarian. Scott's Life Path would have led him to a life of helping others. This number is calculated from reducing his birthdate of 6+27+1956 to nine or less.

Interestingly, the day of Scott's birth (twenty-seven) also reduces to a nine. In some fields of numerology, the day of birth shows the side of self that is often hidden, and only revealed as a person moves into spiritual awareness. Because Scott's Life Path and day of birth are both a nine, he was living his spiritual path for most of his life.

When looking at a Life Path number, you're seeing the work the soul wants to complete during their incarnation.

A Nine Life Path person is empathetic and can be selfless in their giving. They are also tolerant and broad-minded. The red flag of a Nine Life Path is a life so dedicated to others that the Self is ignored.

A person born with the Nine Life Path is typically born into a family where ideas are a primary focus. And no matter how difficult or easy Scott's early years were, by the time he reached adulthood he would have been inspired to help others (and the world) on a grand scale.

In summary, Scott's Life Path represents a person who was on the earth to learn service to mankind. This number is often seen in a person who could jump from one passion to another, taking up the cause of racial injustice one day and saving the whales on another. However, as a Nine Life Path ages, more and more opportunities present themselves to be of service to others. Scott, living at his highest potential, would have been a beacon of light to others.

Scott's Expression

The Expression (or Destiny) number is the sum of the numbers associated with the name at birth—the birth certificate name. It's important to know that the name you are given at birth may change through marriage, nicknames, or even name changes. However, none of those will change the Expression number of your birth name. This number remains with you throughout your lifetime. If you take another name, you do not release the energy of your given name; however, you take on the additional energy of the new name.

The Expression number shows a person's potential and natural abilities. It provides an important clue to the opportunities that life will offer.

When calculating the Expression, don't add the entire name straight through. Calculate each name (first, middle, surname) on its own because knowing the three is important for some of the minor calculations.

Scott 1+3+6+2+2 = 14/5
Douglas 4+6+3+7+3+1+1=25/7
Cunningham 3+3+5+5+9+5+7+8+1+4=50/5
Scott Douglas Cunningham's Expression is 5+7+5=17/8

An eight is the number of ambition and recognition. Success can come easily to an Eight Expression if there's a balance between the physical and the spiritual. The ultimate victory for an Eight Expression is both strength of character and mastery of self.

When the numbers of the Life Path (birthdate) and the Expression are not harmonious, other people may only see the person as represented by their Life Path (nine), not the Expression (eight). This could have been the case with Scott as a Nine Life Path and an Eight Expression can be at odds with one another: The Nine wants the world to be its best while the Eight can be focused only on the practical and the material. These inharmonious numbers would have made it far easier for people to see Scott as a spiritual being without realizing his more practical abilities.

An Eight Expression represents a person who is an explorer, always looking for a way to integrate new ideas with established practices. If an eight is ego-driven, they can act differently just to be noticed. However, a strong eight will mix with unique people who are not afraid of trying new and various ways of accomplishing great things. In this way, Scott's eight would have blended well in his chosen community.

An Eight Expression is also a person who is interested in the unusual, faraway places, as well as the world of publishing (Scott published over twenty books). At heart, an eight is a practical philosopher, seeking to understand the arcane ways of the world's cultures, always drawn to the mystical, but translating them in a practical way that was accessible to anyone.

Scott's Expression would also gift him with exemplary organizational and managerial skills. He would have been capable of handling large projects with ease. However, the negative side of an Eight Expression is a person who is stubborn, as well as impatient with slow progress. An Eight Expression has a quick mind and wants the world to move along at a faster speed.

Scott's Heart's Desire

The Heart's Desire is one of the strongest numbers in numerology because it represents the thing that truly makes a person happy. This number is calculated by adding only the vowels in a person's birth name.

Scott's Heart's Desire was the Master Number Eleven. What made him truly happy? Interacting with others, being an inspiration, and operating throughout life with a keen intuitive sense. A Heart's Desire Eleven wants to be that light in darkness as we saw in his Life Path number.

Elevens can be quite happy living within their own spiritual world. They are ill-suited to the world of "normal business," especially being confined to an office. If they need to work within an office framework, they will be the one person whose approach to work is always unusual and often misunderstood.

Peace, harmony, and community would have held high esteem for Scott. He would have sought out other souls walking a similar path, reacting to an almost unconscious need for forward movement through cooperation. Scott would have avoided crassness, crudeness, or coarseness as he would have seen them as antithetical to his magickal life.

Elevens are so "other-empathetic" that they can become disappointed when "the other" doesn't live up to their expectations. Scott would have seen each person as they *could be*, at their highest potential. If that potential isn't reached, an eleven can feel a deep sense of disappointment. With an Eleven Heart's Desire, Scott would have been drawn to art, music, and beauty in its many forms. He would also have been drawn to teaching, knowing that his spiritual ideals allowed him to see and convey life's mysteries in a way that could reach millions.

Beyond all, the Master Number Eleven is a gift from Spirit. It was Scott's role in his lifetime to return that gift to the world.

I do want to mention that Scott's Minor Heart's Desire was a one. This means that he wanted to accomplish his spiritual and humanitarian goals through a position of leadership.

Scott's Personality

The Personality number is a little like a person's astrological ascendant—it tells us how others see us. In short, it gives us a glimpse into how a person expresses themselves during ordinary circumstances. If just meeting someone, your first impression of them is via their Personality number. This number is calculated by adding the consonants in the birth name. Scott's Personality is a six, the number of the kindly outer self. Abraham Lincoln had the same Personality number.

With a Six Personality number, Scott could easily adjust to any situation in which he found himself. He would have been the person others came to for advice or to gain wisdom. A six is also devoted to family as well as those who are close to them. Relationships, both as a friend or a significant other would have been extremely important to Scott.

While people with a Six Personality can look unassuming, they are not. Their true power is hidden within their Life Path.

Minor Calculations

After calculating the four most important numbers in Scott's name (Life Path, Expression, Heart's Desire, Personality), let's look at some of the minor numbers.

Planes of Expression

The Planes of Expression indicate how a person functions on each plane: Physical, Mental, Emotional, Intuitive. The numbers for each are calculated using these associations. For example, Scott had one "D" and one "M" in his name. Both "D" and "M" are fours, giving him an eight as his physical plane of expression.

Physical	e (5)	w (5)	d (4)	m (4)				
Mental	a (1)	h (8)	j (1)	n (5)	p (7)	g (7)	l (3)	
Emotional	i (9)	o (6)	r (9)	z (8)	b (2)	s (1)	t (2)	x (6)
Intuitive	k (2)	f (6)	q (8)	u (3)	y (7)	c (3)	v (4)	

Physical Plane of Expression: Scott operated on the physical plane as an eight. Again, this is the number of the achiever, the builder. This is the person with a strong vision and the willingness to work hard to make it a reality. On the physical plane, Scott would have been able to accomplish almost anything he desired.

Mental Plane of Expression: Scott operated on the mental plane as a six. With this number, Scott would have easily functioned as a poet and writer. He would also have been a successful artist or teacher. The Mental Six is also a person who never outgrows the need for love.

Emotional Plane: Emotionally, Scott was driven to be of service to humanity as his number on this plane was a nine. He could have had difficulty with relationships if they weren't a part of the world he was creating.

Intuitive Plane: Working on the Intuitive Plane Scott clearly embraced the creativity and originality of the three. The Intuitive Three would also have given him a gift of gab and ideas colored with high imagination.

Karmic Lesson

The Karmic Lesson is calculated by adding the missing numbers in a person's birth name. Because Scott's full name contained the letters for each of the nine numbers, he had no Karmic Lessons.

Life Challenges

During a person's life, they face four challenges. The first is from age zero to thirty, the second age thirty to fifty-five. The third and fourth come later in life. Because Scott crossed to the Otherworld at age thirty-six, he only experienced the first and second challenges.

Scott's First Challenge was that of the number three. This is a period of intense self-criticism and self-doubt. During this time, it's possible that Scott would have doubted the quality of his work or its meaning for others. This is a time of learning your true value in the world.

Although successful, Scott would have doubted himself, oftentimes putting on a happy face when, at heart, he had periods of intense loneliness and self-doubt. Of interest, a Three Challenge is often seen in people with artistic talents.

When Scott returned to Spirit, he was in his Second Challenge, the challenge of the six. This was a time to finally gain a sense of self-satisfaction. It was a time of many opportunities to teach and heal, even as he was leaving his own incarnation. A Six Challenge is also a time of added responsibility, particularly with issues around home, family, and relationships.

Although Scott did not live to experience his third and fourth challenges, both were the challenge of the three—the same challenge he experienced up until age thirty.

Major Stress

In numerology, the Major Stress is found by subtracting the Life Path and the Expression from one another. In this case, Scott's Major Stress would be the number one. One, in this position, represents a person who is torn between focusing on work, on dreaming the next big dream into reality, and feeling forced to be out in the world of leadership.

In some ways, a one stressor gives a person the impetus to be a pioneer—opening new fields of study and development. However, if that person is happy within their own world, being forced into the limelight can carry a stressor that's difficult to deal with. It creates a constant tug-of-war between the inner self and the outer persona.

The Growth Number

The Growth Number is the force that illuminates the best way for a person to expand their development. It's calculated by adding the numbers of the first name.

Scott's Growth Number is five, oftentimes called the most difficult of the numbers. It is the number of travel, change, impermanence, adventure, and restlessness. A five is a challenge to growth because it is the number of the free spirit, and the free spirit does not want to be tied down.

Scott's growth would come from experiencing all of five's faces, from one extreme to another as the fives represent opposite ends of a scale. To grow means avoiding the extremes and doing your best to remain in a more middle ground.

Master Numbers

Because Scott's Heart's Desire was a Master Number, I'd like to share more about it. Eleven is the Master Number of inspiration. If reduced, it becomes a two. If you can imagine the energy of two (unity) vibrating at a higher frequency, you'll understand the energy of eleven. Eleven is a number of idealism, inspiration, and the highest of spiritual ideals. In an ancestral sense, an eleven represents a person born into a family who has gifted you a special talent. Regardless of the nature of the talent, an eleven will use it to make the world a better place.

The Reality Number

The Reality Number is one most easily seen towards the end of life. Although Scott's life was short, he did live the energy of his Reality Number—an eight. This is a life of recognition and authority, underpinned with a unique philosophy. Scott's success as an authority in his field remains even today.

Finding the Way Back Home

From working with the numerology for Scott Cunningham, it's clear that he was a complex man of many skills. Scott's heritage gave him the ability to easily communicate ideas, not a surprise given the prolific nature of his author father, Chet Cunningham. Had Scott not followed a magickal path, it's likely he would have become a writer in another field, most likely taking on the challenge of climate change.

Although highly successful as an author, it's possible Scott spent time feeling torn between his Nine Life Path of helping heal the world, and his desire for worldly success. However, all things being equal, I believe his Heart's Desire was filled to overflowing.

CHAPTER TWO

The 1960s, Magick, and Family Life

CHILDHOOD

In the 1960s, ours was the house on the block where other kids came to play. A long street dead-ended at our house, in the middle of a suburban housing tract that was built in the late-1950s, so it was a good place to play kickball in the street, or to play baseball in our big front yard. Home base was between Dad's den window on the right (facing the house), and Greg and Scott's window on the left. First base was the guy-wire (grounding wire?) from the electrical pole that went into the ground between our house and the one next to us. Second base was the Carrotwood tree in the parking area. Third base was the Chinese Elm tree, near the driveway.

The neighborhood was what my husband calls a bunny hutch, lots of young marrieds with children. We would often get kids from the neighborhood to play with us. As I was so much younger than the rest, I was tolerated on the team only if there weren't enough outfielders. But this training ground is where I learned to hold a bat, hit a ball, kick a ball, and run the bases.

As is often said about those times, we knew to come inside when the streetlights came on. Rarely were we out of sight of our house, situated where it was in the middle of things, so rarely were we called to

Christmas, 1965. From left to right: Scott, Skippy,
Christine, Honey, and Greg.

come to dinner. All Mom had to do was stand in the doorway, and we'd head inside.

There were neighbor birthday parties and adult parties at our house, and neighborhood camp-outs up at our cabin in the Laguna Mountains. Everyone knew everyone else within a twenty-house radius, and everyone's parents felt secure enough to scold everyone's kids when necessary. Sure, we had kid fights. Skinned knees. Bruised arms and "Indian burns." Kids aren't, after all, very nice, or necessarily well-behaved when their parents aren't around. But overall, ours was an amazingly easy childhood, and the neighborhood a fairly contented, easy-going place.

Two exciting things happened to the neighborhood in the early 1970s; a 7-Eleven store was constructed, about a block from our house, and just past it, a post office, where Dad opened up a PO box. Around the same time, a McDonald's opened in the Safeway parking lot, the first one we'd ever seen. Maybe once or twice a year, Dad would go out and bring home McDonald's for dinner.

In 1969, one of my best friends in fourth grade would come over almost every afternoon, and I didn't realize until much later that she did so because my parents were always home. Hers were always at work, and her older sister was also away from the house, either at school, or lessons, or working. At the Cunningham house, my friend had adults she could count on, a snack if she needed it, and companionship that was undemanding. Safety. She didn't tell me all of this until much, much later, after we reconnected as adults, but it has stayed with me.

Dad was a writer. He had a job writing training films for the Navy, but I believe that ended in 1963 or 1964. Before he sold his first Western novel, *Gold Wagon* in 1968, he was selling car columns and wrote articles for anyone who could pay. I know prior to *Gold Wagon*, he had written porn novels under different pseudonyms. Those paid the bills, along with the car columns. I know about the porn novels because we found a couple sacks of them in the attic after he passed away, multiple copies of the same book at times, and only the author would keep those. (Greg and I split the books. I'm not sure where mine are at this point in time.)

Mom was a homemaker, what with three kids to ride herd over. So having them both at home gave us kids a sense of security that made everything so easy.

Dinner was, of course, always at five thirty PM. Between Greg and Scott, dinner was often full of laughter and stories. I remember, more than once, they had my mom laughing so hard she had tears running down her cheeks. And when we had a guest for dinner, usually another kid, those stories that kept us in stitches were ramped up.

In the summertime, having dinner at five thirty and then cleaning up—when I was younger, I cleared the table, and Greg and Scott took turns either washing or drying the dishes—meant more playing outside after dinner. When I was older, we all three rotated kitchen chores. Often the person who dried dishes let them air-dry. A trick that would have worked if someone hadn't noticed and kept sprinkling the dishes in the dish drainer with water . . . cough Greg cough.

We'd play Hide n' Go Seek, Capture the Flag, kickball. Hopscotch for me, and roller skating. Basketball, if Dad moved the car. All the neighbor kids ran wild and free. The boogeyman didn't exist, and the world was a safe place.

Years later, I had separate conversations with both Scott and Greg about this very thing, because all of a sudden it seemed there were predators everywhere, and to my shock, always had been everywhere. Were we really that happy a family? Yes, we were. Was our neighborhood really that safe? Yes, it was. Were our parents really that nice? Yes, they were. Our parents didn't drink, smoke, yell at us, or swear, but they did have that patented look of parental disappointment down when we'd earned it. They were both college graduates with wide areas of interest.

Were there kids in our neighborhood who were being molested, and we didn't know about it? Probably. Were there drunks who beat their kids, and we didn't know about it? Again, probably. But looking back, we didn't see those things when we were kids. That doesn't mean they weren't there; it just means we weren't personally impacted by them.

We had a circle of cement in the backyard that held a tetherball pole in the wintertime. In summer, the pole and tetherball would be put away, and Dad would put up a Doughboy pool, maybe thirty inches tall and I think eight feet in diameter. We'd play Marco Polo in the pool, and Scott rarely was "it" because he was difficult to catch.

Around 1965 the three of us took swimming lessons. A neighbor on a street north and to the west of ours had a built-in, as we called them then, an in-ground pool. She was probably a member of our church, the San Carlos United Methodist Church, and was a certified swim instructor. Dad signed us all up. The first year, we were driven there. But a year later, the summer I was six, the three of us walked to her house for classes, a few blocks away. I'll always remember her house for the striking black and white paint job on it.

In 1966 Dad had a fireplace installed in the house, along the same wall where the kitchen window was (but, you know, in the living room). He had that living room window taken out, and the fireplace put in. The brick face was of fossils, a brick that I think was called shell limestone, which came from Texas. The bricks measured four inches by twelve inches and were a pretty cream color. Dad added a built-in bench around the fireplace of the same shell limestone, covered in black slate and deep enough for seating. My mother bought red square cushions for the sides, and they stayed there for years until they wore out.

Though only two years apart, Greg and Scott were very different from each other. Greg was into cars and guitars. Scott was a reader, a piano player, and an observer. We would tease each other, torment each other, try to beat each other at board games, but we were family.

Stratego, Probe, Monopoly, Hearts, Canasta, and Solitaire were just some of the games we played.

Here's one of Greg's memories:

There was one time, in the early days, when the three of us were all reading in the living room. The television set was on, but none of us were paying attention. Dad stood in the doorway for a while, just watching. Finally, he spoke.

"Whoever wrote those books you're reading should be proud that their stories can hold your attention. Whoever wrote the TV show should be embarrassed."

Well, he wasn't wrong.

Greg is six years older than me, and Scott four years older. When I came along, the only girl, I was cherished and doted upon, and was definitely Daddy's girl. Scott and I were in grade school together for three years at John H. Forward Elementary School, before he went on to Pershing Junior High, leaving me behind. Both schools were within easy walking distance. Greg was in the first sophomore class, and a part of the first class to begin, and graduate from, the brand-new Patrick

Henry High School (sophomore through senior), a bus ride away. It was built to handle up to two thousand kids. When I graduated from Patrick Henry in January of 1978, we had over four thousand students, and a split day schedule had been implemented to handle the overflow.

Scott was not a stereotypical middle child. He was not a peacemaker. He was an observer. He went his own way. He had no desire to compete with Greg, with his interest in cars and guitars and rock 'n roll, and he pretty much ignored me when I was younger.

He wasn't the jokester when he was young, though as an adult, he enjoyed punning, as any of his friends will tell you. When we were kids, he tended toward the serious, though he was quick-witted enough to riff on a joke. He started wearing glasses around the age of ten, which merely added to the serious air he gave off when he was in observation mode. I wasn't aware of it at the time, but wearing glasses at such a young age also made him a target at school.

Mainly, he watched, learned, and became absorbed by how things worked. Science and the stars, going to the moon, and the plants that grew in forests or on cliffs were things he explored, were what held his interest. He took a fascination for Dad's mimeograph machine and helped whenever Dad needed to make multiple copies of flyers, or when our family Christmas letter needed to be copied. (Oh, the scent of mimeograph ink!)

Coming across the country at a very young age also left a mark on him, as the landscape unfolded through the car window. He saw the rolling plains, the mountains, and finally the ocean, and every new vista was a point of fascination for him, even though he was only a three-year-old.

He read a lot (well, we all did) and practiced piano every day. Apparently, he participated in a lot of piano competitions when he was younger, which I didn't remember until I went through Dad's papers, years after Scott's death. I wonder if that was because I was just so self-absorbed, to not know about his competitions? I don't ever remember going to one of them. Maybe I was too young?

As a young one, I was pretty much on my own . . . well, me and Mom. The boys were in school by the time I was aware of more than eating and pooping and crawling. The one vivid memory I have from that early time is from 1962. Grandma Lola Loit came to live with us late in the year. As far as I remember, Grandma Loit was my mother's father's maternal grandmother, my great-great-grandmother (but I could be wrong about that, ha!). They put her in "my" bedroom, and the parents moved my crib into the boys' room. They had bunk beds, which made room for my crib.

One night, I was standing up in my crib talking to my brothers, and they started making walking noises, slapping their hands on the bed, as if someone was coming down the hallway. I'm pretty sure Greg was the ringleader, though Scott quickly chimed in, too.

Christmas with Grandma Loit, 1962.

"Lay down, Chrissy. Mom and Dad are coming."

Heart thundering, I laid back down. Nothing. I got back up and started talking. The slapping sounds started up again.

"Chrissy. Lay down. Mom and Dad."

I laid down, still unsure. Waited a bit, then popped back up. Talked a little louder this time.

"They're really coming down the hallway now, Chrissy. Lay down, I'm not kidding!"

But by that time, I'd had enough.

"Nuh unh, they are not."

Of course, my parents did come that last time, and my brothers busted a gut laughing at me as the parents scolded me for keeping my brothers awake.

They teased me about that for, well, years.

Grandma Loit came to us at the end of her life. It is my belief that she died in my bedroom, though I have no memory of that nor, indeed, any confirmation of it from outside sources. Just a Christmas photo with her, and a mention of her living with us in the Christmas letter my dad always wrote. Then, nothing. No more mention of her in subsequent Christmas letters, not even to tell people she died. Perhaps there were very few left who even knew or remembered her, and that was why? I don't know. This is just one of many things I wish I could ask Dad about, but of course it's far too late now.

Another memory, maybe after Grandma Loit passed away. It was summer, still morning. The screen door was somehow unlatched, and at three-something years old, I walked outside into the front yard, where I was not allowed by myself. But life beckoned, so I went.

I was barefoot, wearing, I think, a new sundress that mom had made. I walked across the grass, and I remember how it felt as though the earth was breathing underneath my feet, the grass tickling me. I got to the sidewalk, out from under the shade of the elm tree.

The concrete was already very warm. The sun was bright overhead. Doves cooed on the power lines above me, the air smelled sweet, and for just a moment, I *knew* all the possibilities ahead of me for my life—all the amazing, wonderful, exciting things to come, and a sort of ecstasy came over me, my heart bursting with joy, and love, and happiness.

I knew, somehow, that everything was going to work out just fine. That I was safe. That I was loved. That I was cared for, and that when the time came, I would care for myself.

I heard my mother call me, and I ran into the house on chubby legs, breathless with knowledge and power and belief, but my three-year-old self didn't have the words then to tell her. I remember throwing my arms up in the air. She picked me up and hugged me.

"Chrissy, what is it?"

I remember putting my hands on her cheeks and touching my nose to hers the way we used to do. But only one word came out of my mouth, because my heart was too full.

"Love."

Mom beamed at me and forgot to scold me for being outside by myself.

And of course, the memory of what I had seen, what I knew, faded swiftly.

It came flooding back to me after Dad died in 2017, when I stood on that same piece of sidewalk that he would never walk again, and I lifted my face to the sun.

I don't remember what that little girl saw. But I remember how she felt. And it's how I still feel. Everything is going to work out just fine.

I am loved and blessed by the Universe, as we truly all are. Greg, Scott, and I won the family lottery. Our parents were so supportive, loving, and by all the gods—it was a safe home. It wasn't until long after I moved away that I realized how blessed we all were.

I must have been six or maybe seven. We were in the living room playing a board game, sitting around the coffee table, at the end of a hot summer day. Mom was in the kitchen, getting dinner ready, and Dad was, naturally, in his den, writing. I'm not sure which brother started it, but this time it was probably Scott.

"Chrissy, you have B.O."

"No, I don't. Stupid."

Greg laughed. "Yes, you do. B.O."

Supremely irritated (because I was the princess of the family, dontcha know), I glared at them both.

"What does B.O. even mean?"

"Body odor. You stink."

"I do not. MOOOOOM!"

"Yes, honey?" Mom, in the kitchen, making dinner.

"What does B.O. mean?"

"It means body odor, honey." She kept her voice cool and matter of fact.

The boys busted up laughing. I think I gave up playing whatever game we were playing and stomped off in a huff. Today, I'm quite sure Mom had heard everything and was stifling her laughter, but back then I wasn't aware.

In retrospect, it's funny as hell.

Scott was always different; like I said, not the stereotypical middle child, not the peacemaker. No, not Scott. He didn't try to best Greg; he simply wasn't interested in the competition. He didn't make peace, because we were a fairly peaceful bunch to begin with.

He pretty much ignored me when I was younger, unless it was family time, or he was bored and wanted someone to play with. My parents called him their "sensitive and shy" child when he was young. Dad called him Tiger.

He knew he was different. Around the same time as the body odor episode, which would make him ten, he went for some "testing" that Mom and Dad looked serious about. It turned out he went in for IQ testing, as he told me years later.

Scott was smart. It came out in his questions, his interests, his discussions, his vocabulary, his reading, and I suppose my parents were curious. It wasn't that he was the best student, because he wasn't. My parents loved that I got mostly As and Bs on my report card (mainly because I was terrified to fail), and I know that Scott stayed in the B and C range of things. My guess is that it felt safe there for him, but that's only a guess. No, there must have been another reason Scott went in for testing, and at this point in time, that reason is gone.

He was an outlier, even in the family. Always and forever curious. Always reading, but not always fiction. Always creating something, and in that respect was quite like Grandma Hazel.

Hazel Zedicher married Merle Cunningham, a farmer, when she was not even twenty. She knew little to nothing about being a farmer's wife and being the baby of her family with three older siblings, she knew even less about raising children; but she raised three kids, two boys and a girl, and made do with helping hands from neighbors and her own brothers and sisters. She sewed many of the family's clothes. Once her three children were out of the house, she turned her talents to making dolls, stuffed animals, aprons, holiday decorations, anything that she could then sell at the local consignment shop under her brand, "Cottage Creations." She was a quilter and made sure every grandchild had a quilt of their own, from babyhood to adulthood.

Scott wasn't a regular sewer or doll maker, but he enjoyed creating "sets." One year, after the family's first trip to Disneyland, he re-created parts of the *Pirates of the Caribbean* ride in one part of the big L-shaped planter on the patio. There was a cardboard treasure chest with lots of gold and jewels spilling out of it. He also created parts of *It's a Small World* on the other part of the planter, with the funny trees and big flowers. He walked us through it, and even the neighbor children came to see. I believe he charged a penny per person if they chose to see the ride in the wagon, which he pulled. One customer per ride.

In his teens, he dipped candles, made incense, became intensely curious about growing plants. His quest for knowledge led him far and wide, and from his initial correspondence with people he did not know, he began friendships that lasted him his entire life.

When he was older and living on his own, he was wary of new people. He could seem cold, or aloof, if he didn't know you, if he couldn't put you into a slot of sorts. I'm saying this wrong, but until he knew you accepted him for who he was, he could seem quite abrupt and kind of unfriendly, when in actuality he was just being shy and protective.

Greg was the funnyman in the family, and Scott would riff off of Greg's prompts. Until I was twelve or so, we had dinner together as a family every night. To prevent inter-kid wrangling, we sat at an oval dining table pushed against the big window at the end of the galley-style kitchen. Scott was in one window-corner, Greg the other, with me in the middle, and Mom between Greg and me, and Dad between me and Scott.

Whenever one of us used a word that we weren't completely sure of the meaning or made a reference to something we didn't fully understand, Dad sent us to either the dictionary or the set of encyclopedias that graced the bookcase between my room and the boys' room.

Our conversations at dinner were wide-ranging and interesting, and always, always supportive. Quite often funny. We were encouraged to talk about our day at school, and when we were young, we jumped at the chance to be in the spotlight. As we grew older, not everything that happened during our day was discussed, as is natural.

In September of 1966, a new TV show came on, and our parents decided they'd let us watch it. So even though *Star Trek* came on after my normal bedtime, I was allowed to watch. We all loved it. I believe it's the only show we all watched together, every time it came on.

Later in that decade, Scott and I watched Rowan and Martin's *Laugh-In*; Carol Burnett's variety show; after school, it was *Gilligan's Island*, *Green Acres*, *Petticoat Junction*. And always, we watched cartoons on a Saturday morning.

Dinners together changed when I started going to ballet classes six days a week in 1974. Greg had already married and moved out; Scott had graduated high school, so he was out and about with various jobs while he still lived at home. I ate whenever I got home, usually well after Mom and Dad had eaten dinner. Mom was often there to talk to me about my day, and as I got older that wasn't always what I wanted. I know that as a young teen, I veered between worrying about Mom and being totally exasperated with her. It seemed to me she lived half a life; but no one can know how another person lives. Not truly. Not even when you're in the same house.

Plus, Mom went through a second menopause. She'd had a hysterectomy due to fibroids when she was thirty-five, and at that time, went through a medically-induced menopause; but then eight years later, she went through another, physical menopause. She was also on experimental medication for multiple sclerosis. All this, at the same time I was going through puberty. Yeah, fun times at our house during those years.

From reading his biography I know that Scott spent many nights out of the house, often coming home after two in the morning. To my knowledge, he was never given a curfew, nor was he ever scolded about whenever he came home, unlike me. Dad always waited up for him, however, something Scott told me years later.

SCOTT, MAGICK, AND ME

As a teenager, Scott taught me how to enter into a trance state (it involved staring at a wall and letting my eyes go blurry, as I remember—I've improved greatly on that early beginning), and to set my intention and see myself succeeding at whatever my heart was set on. At thirteen, I was still very involved with the San Carlos United Methodist Church, a part of the Sacred Dance group that our minister's wife started. I was also fascinated with Scott's divination, trance states, and pretty much everything he did, though we did not spend much time together. He was working and going to school, and I was finishing school and going to ballet class. While many people would see church and divination interests as being at odds, it just seemed normal to me. Unfortunately, a lot of what he taught me went by the wayside as I found my feet as a ballet dancer. There was little time to do anything other than school, homework, and dance.

The incense he lit at night would waft out his window at the front of the house and come into my window at the side of the house, filling my dreams. At the time, I had no idea he was creating his own incense blends and writing down his recipes, but I firmly believe this is where my love of incense began.

Scott was the first person to give me the nickname "Legs" back when I was twelve, and the only one to use it. I miss him with every breath I take.

It has been said by his friends that he could use anything as a divination tool; the way the cheese bubbled on a pizza, for instance, or how cream looked when poured into a cup of coffee before stirring. He was quite accurate, from what I've been told; so much so that I believe he had psychic abilities.

I had forgotten about his ease with divination until I reread *Whispers of the Moon*, David Harrington and deTraci Regula's biography of Scott. Way back when, he used to use one of Mom's white cereal bowls filled with water. He'd put a couple drops of baby oil in the water, then add a couple of drops of ink, and scry. Most often he'd do that in the kitchen, rather than his bedroom, which is why I remember it; and he always had a notebook handy for notes.

If it was cloudy outside, Scott would search the skies. At the beach, he'd read the way seaweed clumped or stretched across a section of damp sand. The number of crows in the sky held meaning for him; the rhythm of the doves cooing did as well, and so did the dance of the hummingbirds, and the number of butterflies in the garden. Absolutely everything in Nature was magickal for him. I remember one period, in the mid-1970s, where Scott was fascinated with divination of all sorts, and shared many styles with me. The one I remember best is when he showed me how to use a pendulum to answer questions. He didn't have anything fancy. I think he tied a bit of string to the head of a nail and used that. Metaphysical shops weren't a thing back then, and any that did exist were certainly not within walking distance.

One time, I walked by him in the kitchen and saw him gazing into a bowl of water, a dark blue bottle of food coloring nearby. Since we'd been doing the divination stuff, instead of snarking about him not cleaning the stove like Mom had asked him to, I asked him what he saw.

He smiled, mentioned something about seeing me washing dishes that night, and I left in a huff. Which was, I assume, his intention.

Every time we had a fire in the fireplace, or had one while camping, he'd see things in the flames, and encourage me to do so. This is a practice I still do, to this day. Our family attraction to fire made fire gazing a familiar pastime. Back in the 1960s, at any family campsite (usually a trip to Oregon to see our grandparents and other relatives), after setting up the huge, heavy canvas tent, Greg and Scott were sent off to look for kindling for the evening fire. Downed branches only.

Once they were back, Dad would remind us how to build a fire in the available fire ring. A crumple of paper, if we had it (which we usually did, as Dad would buy a newspaper each day when we were traveling), then a cone of tiny twigs and dry pine needles. On top of that, bigger kindling. Then add flame.

After the kindling was truly lit, he would add the bigger pieces of wood, trying not to smother the little fire. Once the flames grew big and the fire steady, we'd gather around and just stare at its beauty, feeding it more kindling, moving it around. We all learned to love the fire pit from our camping days. When it dwindled to coals, we'd bring out the sticks and marshmallows, the graham crackers and chocolate bars, and make s'mores. Now that I think about it, I bet Scott checked the pattern of the burn on the marshmallow for signs. To this day, the scent of a campfire on the night air is soothing, and I feel those long gone around me once more.

A couple years after Scott's death, I walked into a metaphysical store on Lankershim Boulevard in North Hollywood, and smelled Super Hit incense for the first time. That's when I realized how much I missed incense. That smell reminds me of home and Scott, and I have incorporated it into my life ever since, though I have no way of knowing if he ever used Super Hit, or if it was available back then. I mostly light Super Hit or nag champa. Both are such reassuring scents to me that I tend to take them with me when I travel, though to my dismay, hotels typically prohibit incense.

I light incense when I have a fire outside in the fire pit. I light incense when I'm writing, when I'm sad, when I need the comfort of scent. Without Scott's early and unintended influence, I might never have fallen so hard for incense.

I wish he had taught me, oh, so much more than he did. I wish I had thought to ask. But I do have his books, and they are a comfort.

Let's speak of his books again for a moment. When I first read *Wicca: A Guide for the Solitary Practitioner*, it felt like I was seeing Scott's heart and soul for the very first time. He writes in a voice I never heard, but it felt like him. It felt like his authentic voice that I was hearing for the first time.

When I read his *Book of Shadows*, published in 2009, I see the scholar in him. Seeing his handwriting makes me smile with recognition. Reading the correspondences informs my own growing knowledge. And while apparently some people say his correspondences are "wrong," I'll just say that when he was first learning, the internet wasn't a thing. Knowledge was handed down, person to person; books were checked out of the library if they carried them, or purchased with allowance money, or later, money that probably should have gone to pay a bill.

Scott's first few books were written on a hand-me-down Selectric III typewriter, and the drafts of his appendices and bibliographies were all first done by hand. Writers in the metaphysical craft world today are fortunate, indeed, to have the internet and computers at the tips of their fingers.

Scott is practical, funny, and kind in his writing. He speaks to your soul and tells you that whatever you feel the need to do or change with a spell, do it. Any time I need to reconnect with him, I pick up one of his books, and I can hear him speaking to me. I know he has that effect on other people . . . whoever reads his books feels like he is talking just to them. It's a gift of his and I am so grateful for it.

When Scott became interested in plants, he asked Dad for a bit of the garden. (Timeframe—mid-'70s.) Dad gave him the far back left corner on the embankment, which had been built up with a short brick wall. Scott planted prickly pear cactus, rosemary, crown-of-thorns, and other plants. The other plants all died out, but the cactus, rosemary, and crown-of-thorns remained there in the corner, right up to when Greg and I sold the house in 2017. Those plants lived for over forty years. Dad tended them, watered them, pruned them, and refused to dig them up. In retrospect, perhaps it was his way of honoring Scott, the person he was, the man who died before any of us were ready.

Scott grew many plants in pots, first in the Orange Avenue apartment, and then in greater numbers at the apartment closer to my parents. He always, always, grew rosemary and lavender. I feel he grew rosemary as a way to be closer to Mom, since her first name is Rose Marie. Scott and Mom had a close relationship. He was gentle and loving with her, took her to the movies and shopping, and did what he could to help her out.

Dad had taken many of Scott's plants to his house, those that weren't given away when Scott moved in with them. One of the plants was a succulent of some sort that reproduces when its leaves drop and root. We've tried to figure out the name of it but keep coming up empty.

Dad's side yard was full of these plants in his later years. In 2016, I was given a few plants, and after Dad died, I took a few more. Now they are in my garden, descended from the plants Scott had grown, so long ago. For that reason alone, I would cherish them, but they're also pretty cool.

Protection of the Snapdragon

By Amie Emberharte

Scott Cunningham set me free with the words he wrote. Though our physical paths never crossed in this lifetime, I met Scott through his pages at a party in 1992. I was new in town and had recently met a potential new voice teacher who just happened to be a Wiccan High Priest. He invited me to a dinner party to introduce me to some of his friends, recommended a local tarot reader, and spent time sharing his experience and answering my endless questions. A whole new world was opening in front of me where people embraced the mystical and magickal as real things rather than childish imaginings.

A well-worn copy of *Encyclopedia of Magical Herbs* sat on top of a basket full of interesting books next to my friend's favorite chair. It caught my eye immediately. What was intended to be a fast glance quickly became a need to dig into all the juicy, magickal details of herbs, plants, and flowers. During the dinner party, we talked about Scott Cunningham, magickal plants, and covens, and enjoyed a wonderful dinner. I left that night with much to consider and a borrowed *Encyclopedia of Magical Herbs*.

The words and pictures on each page transported me back in time to my childhood home in the country and even before then to places distant before this lifetime. In misty montage, memories surfaced and danced on the movie screen of my mind's eye. First, I was gathering indigo for making dye in some distant time with a sense of gratitude and connection to the plant. I was watching myself harvest it intentionally and with great devotion to the work. Then pecans were being carefully shelled by my grandmother's hands for holiday pies and the potential magick present when we ate what I now call Prosperity Pie. The peonies growing in great abundance around the house were planted for their beauty and fragrance, but at further glance, perhaps they provided protection too? Then there was my mother. She loved plants of all kinds and made our little homestead into a magical place without it being intentionally magical at all. I could distinctly remember the hundred times she called my little brother and me out of her flower beds and away from her snapdragons.

It was mesmerizing to flip through the pages and read Scott's words about the protection of the snapdragon and remember how we would sit in the large beds all around the front of the house, opening and closing their fiery mouths. As children, perhaps we somehow knew their magick and intuitively played guarding the castle of our home.

There is a special energy and presence to connecting with others on sacred ground of any kind, and I cherish it. There is also deep healing for me in solitary practice. I had been singing my spiritual solo in whispered tones and notes for so long, hiding away from prying eyes and opinionated minds, lest they steal my cherished existence from me. I was and am a mystic . . . a seeker of direct connection with Nature and the Divine this entire lifetime. The desire is not manufactured or conjured; it is innate and was amplified through the tragic beauty of my near-death experience as a child. In those few moments across the veil, I experienced more than the fundamentalist pictures my relatives and most of their churches painted. So much more.

I knew my very bones in all their natural glory and every breath and expression of Nature held secrets, power, illumination, truth, and divinity.

Living after coming back into my body, I knew what it was to be connected from within to the Divine . . . to walk with one foot here on soil and the other touching the edge of a Heaven that smelled and tasted vastly different than the descriptions offered to me by my relatives. I could see the Beyond in little places and moments all day, every day. I wanted to share and celebrate all that I had seen and heard, and the way the echoes of the Beyond reverberated here on Earth and within every living thing. Unfortunately, that didn't fit into the box of acceptable things in the households where I grew up. So, I sat at a proverbial table for one, drinking it all in and wondering at being so alone in my perceptions, because every "witchy" thing was simply not allowed.

I looked around and found whispers everywhere. Divinity lived in the trees and the wind in their branches and the sound of leaves rustling in my ears harmonized with bird song. In thunder rolling across midwestern skies punctuated with lightning bolts, I felt the exclaiming electrified messages. My heart reverberated with the vibration of deities various and many, and they were all too big to fit in the smallness of a primordial father ruling the Universe from one tiny throne in another world far away. My beliefs were heresy, demon possession, and reason enough to shun me without a second thought.

I spent many years simply following my intuition and experiences even when doing so ruffled the feathers of my extended family and community. I lived and learned a lot. You see, to those who raised me, everything I did was all absolutely unacceptable. From the way I wore my hair, to the dead people I talked to and played with when I knew the grownups weren't looking, just about everything I did was deemed damnable. My relatives offered absolutes where I saw ebb and flow. They demanded sacrifice of self and self-expression while I was busy noticing and celebrating all the beautiful little idiosyncrasies of every human I knew. They saw sin in the babies I rocked in the nursery, while all I could see was a small piece of the Eternal waking up and exploring brand new skin.

There was another way. There had to be. How could I live denying the essence of my existence? So, I packed up my knapsack like The Fool in the Tarot and took the leap of faith. I chose to follow my own way even though it meant leaving much of the external familiar behind.

"Amie, you know you can do this work privately, right? You don't have to join a coven if you don't want to, and besides, you've always been magical. You're already on the path and you just don't know it yet."

It's funny how a question and an observation from a friend can change your life. The simple answer was . . . no. I had no idea.

Then came the words Scott had the gumption and courage to write after spending sixteen years working, researching, and experiencing this path less traveled! When I picked up *Wicca: A Guide for the Solitary Practitioner* at the direction of a friend in a Pagan bookstore and read through the preface, I felt I had found more than a map. I had found a guide and friend. Scott believed I was on to something. He believed in the power of personal connection with divinity, and he legitimized the magnetism of what I came to understand was my practice and the amazing experiences it produced. Scott believed me. His words told me he did. He helped me feel less alone in under three pages of printed words. Then he went on to share much more than I knew, and he answered soul-deep questions and filled in gaps with missing pieces. It was all written to give me ways to live and work in my solitary way.

Scott's writing feels somehow familiar to me. In those many early days of digging through myself to sort out and heal the brainwashing and spiritual abuse I experienced, it was amazing to read Scott's books. Chapter after chapter was filled with the validation I needed in order to trust myself, my intuition, and life. Spiritual attunement and connection with Nature became increasingly important, and Scott provided encouragement and direction in simple, attainable, and natural ways that resonated with me.

I appreciate and love Scott more with each reading of every page, and I am surely not the only one. This is why our creations are so important! It inspires me to think of the web still being woven from his body of work and how many lives he continues to touch. His legacy is profound. It speaks of living one's own truth with increasing fullness and the importance of sharing with and teaching others. Scott had quite a bit of influence in swinging open the broom-closet doors and doing it all in ways that encourage us to do the same.

THE PARENTS

How can I possibly describe our parents? Let me start with our dad, Chet Cunningham. Dad was a gentle soul who rarely got angry. He was courteous and kind to almost everyone he met. He could be stern, but it never seemed a bad thing; we were never afraid of him, but we did fear his disappointment. Dad was rarely awake before eight in the morning; we never saw him before school. In later years, the only time he'd be up early would be to call his editors in New York City.

The highlight of Dad's life was most likely during the late 1970s, early 1980s when Scott learned to write novels, there in the den that had always been Dad's refuge.

To help Dad and to make some cash, Scott had taken over Dad's car columns. I think he was seventeen or maybe eighteen. He'd write brief columns about tires, or brakes, or how to handle a car during a skid, and then Dad would sell them to car dealerships who then ran them as ad space in local newspapers. Before Scott took over, for a couple decades Dad had these columns all over the country, all running basically the same verbiage, just changing the dealership's name. For that reason, Dad would only sell to one dealership in each county.

Scott would spend half of his day at Dad's, writing in the den that Dad worked in. This arrangement pleased Dad and made him very proud. They became colleagues, able to speak each other's language. When he went home in the evenings (sometimes after dinner, which made Mom happy), Scott would work on his first non-fiction book, which became *Earth Power*, published in 1983.

When they would take breaks, Scott and Dad would go out into the garden and work there together. I truly think this was the happiest time for Dad, and I know Scott was grateful for the chance to learn and also to keep an eye on our parents.

Many authors have said they only write four hours a day—Hemingway, for example. My dad would call that out for himself as being lazy. He did more than writing each day, though. Mornings were for editing what he wrote the night before. Afternoons were for either writing car columns or doing marketing for those columns, until Scott took that over. Evenings were for fresh writing, until the news at eleven, and then Johnny Carson after. Oh, how he mourned when Johnny retired. No one took his place in Dad's heart. But knowing he was up until after midnight during the week made it understandable that he wasn't up before eight in the morning. Dad's writing work ethic made a deep impression on Scott.

Until 1983, when he bought his TRS-80 computer, Dad wrote on a typewriter. He'd use carbon paper in order to always have two complete copies of his work. He loved his Selectric III, as it had a memory chip that would hold nine pages. All his chapters during that time, until his TRS-80 and beyond, were nine pages long. In the early years, Mom would edit him and sometimes would re-type his work for him; but by the mid-1980s, her control wasn't that good anymore, so she would edit by hand. When he bought another computer a couple years later, Scott was gifted the TRS-80.

By contrast, I didn't truly start writing until 2001, and at Dad's urging, finally joined the Romance Writers of America in 2002. That meant I always had a computer at my fingertips. I've always had the internet for research available to me. Well, there was that one book I tried to write when I was nineteen, and I did use a typewriter for that . . . but as that was so long ago now, I tend to forget about that attempt.

My first novel didn't get published until after my mother passed away, and I realized I needed to get serious about writing. My first paranormal romance book was published in 2011, with two more books in the series published thereafter. My first contemporary romance series was published in 2014–2016; that series includes a short Christmas romance and three full-length novels.

Chet's garden was his other passion. He used to water the yard, or weed, and work out book plots or issues. Now, mind you, he didn't seem to have the plot problems I do. His characters always did just what he told them to do. When I asked him his secret to plotting, he folded a regular piece of typing paper into thirds.

"Up here, this top section, is your first act. This middle section is your second act. The third section? Third act and end of show. That's it, that's all. Don't overcomplicate it or overthink it, Chrissy."

This is advice that I often go back to when I get stuck. I'm not saying it always works for me, but it is a comfort to fall back on this trick every now and then.

The only way I can describe our mom Rose Marie Cunningham is to say she was sunshine and sweetness. Innately kind, an avid lover of gardens until it just became too much for her, and a fair cook, Mom was always there with a hug, or a cookie, or a story whenever life became a bit too much.

To Dad, she was a bright flame, a sparkling mind, and an agile body. Watching those things he loved about her decline as multiple sclerosis took her over was one of the worst parts of his life.

Mom loved oil paints. She painted several paintings over the years until she couldn't control the paintbrush anymore. I own a few of her paintings. She wanted to teach special ed kids, and she went back to school for her teaching certificate while I was in my teens. She did actually work as a substitute teacher in special ed for the school district until she couldn't safely drive any longer. She wanted to sing in the church choir, and she did, for years and years, even after she needed a wheelchair because she couldn't stand long enough to sing. She was in the choir until her eyes couldn't follow the words on the page fast enough so her brain could tell her what to sing. (I just read that in one of her journals.) She was horribly conflicted about staying in the choir when she felt she couldn't keep up. She wanted to write, so she put together a small booklet of sayings and prayers that she gave to family and friends. She was an active member of the P.E.O. Sisterhood and the San Carlos United Methodist Church.

She loved baking cookies and cakes for us. One of our favorite cookies was called *Gigantor* cookies—a type of Ranger cookie that she'd make really big (think five-inch cookies). There was a cartoon on in the early-1960s called *Gigantor* that the boys loved to watch, and she named the cookies after the show.

She also loved reading. I started reading romance because of her copy of Rosemary Rogers's *Sweet Savage Love*, stuffed in the cushions of her chair. I picked it up and started reading—I believe I was fourteen.

Dad was the writer, but Mom was the storyteller. When I was in grade school, she told me the best bedtime stories, ones filled with fairies, and magical bunnies who didn't know how to make Easter eggs and who needed the help of a special little girl. She told me of far-away places that were tucked under the flowers in our garden, and all about the wee folk who lived there. It was a magical time, and she would re-tell my favorites.

Mom was always up very early, and by the time I got up for school, she was dressed neatly and had her makeup done. Quite the '50s housewife, her style was Laura Petrie from *The Dick Van Dyke Show*, neat trousers and a blouse rather than pearls, skirts, and heels. For that matter, by the time I was six or so, she couldn't wear heels anymore, and she rarely wore the pearls Dad had given her for their wedding. She went to the hairdresser once a week, and once every month she'd get a perm and color. Her hair was dyed red, which is why I went red when I decided to color my hair back in the early 1980s. It's a good color on both of us.

At some point when I was in grade school, Mom decided she was going to get into shape, so she tried to jog slowly around the block. She ended up spraining both ankles, so to say she wasn't the best of athletes would be putting it mildly. (This, however, was a pain point for Dad, as they had been quite active for the first ten years of their marriage.)

Dad took care of her until she could walk easily again. He always took care of her. Always. This is something I will reiterate, as so often men walk away from wives who have physical issues. And yes, women also walk away when their husbands have physical issues—but it seems to me to be rarer that a woman walks away. I admit to being possibly exceedingly wrong on this point.

When Scott was about two, the family still lived in Royal Oak, Michigan. One cold winter night, Rosie and Chet went to the movies, having secured a babysitter for Greg and Scott. The movie over, they stepped outside into the chilly Michigan winter, and almost immediately one half of Rosie's face drooped, as if all the muscles there just stopped working.

After much testing, and an initial diagnosis of encephalomyelitis, the doctor sat both my parents down and told them to move to a moderate climate. Somewhere that doesn't get too hot and doesn't get too cold.

After a diligent search, Chet found a job as a training film writer at Convair San Diego, so they made plans to move. At my mother's last neurology appointment before they left Michigan, almost two years after her diagnosis, her doctor told her that they didn't know what caused what she had, and they didn't know if it was hereditary. Therefore, since she already had two beautiful boys, it would be best if she didn't have any more children. She smiled, nodded, and left his office, not bothering to tell her husband what the doctor said, because she dearly wanted to have another child—and she thought she might be pregnant. In late June of 1959, they piled into their light blue Ford Fairlane, and headed west. Rosie decided then that if her baby lived, she would name it either Christopher or Christine, as a nod to Christianity, and a thank you to God.

When they got to San Diego, they rented a house until they could find one to buy. Input from my brother Greg, who would have been not-quite-six at the time:

"We lived in a rented house in Lemon Grove, on Skyline Drive, before we got the house in San Carlos. I broke a neighbor's window playing baseball there and had to tell Dad about it, only he wasn't at his typewriter. I had to talk to him while he was shaving in the bathroom, in the middle of the day, for some reason known only to him."

After weeks of diligent looking, Chet and Rosie found and bought a house, still under construction, in a brand-new housing tract in the new suburb of San Carlos. They moved in on October 6, 1959, with no electricity and no running water (but that got connected within a matter of days). For years, we celebrated every October 6th by eating dinner by candlelight and cooking on camp stoves.

My parents' love seems so deep to me, as I look back. We never saw them argue. (Downside of that is, I never learned how to argue with someone I love. I'm still working on it.) We also never were in doubt that we were loved, unconditionally. They didn't push any of us in any one direction. Neither of my parents used swear words around us. They didn't drink or smoke. They gave parties for adults, where they would play word games and board games. There was always lots of food, lots of sodas, lots of guests, and no alcohol, ever. There was always lots of laughter, and kids were most welcome. When someone did bring over a bottle, Dad would thank them kindly, put it high up in a cupboard, and much later, either toss it or give it away to friends of his that did indulge.

Greg and I do drink, wine and beer mostly, with cocktails for me. Scott smoked cigarettes like a fiend, especially when on a deadline, but was a lightweight when it came to alcohol, from what I have been told. We never drank together, though, so I don't know. Oh, and Scott never smoked in front of Mom and Dad, or me for that matter. He also never smelled like cigarette smoke around us. Now that's magick!

Later, parties or just family get-togethers included playing a game of pool. In the '70s, one of Dad's big purchases was a pool table. Dad loved pool and taught all of us kids how to play. Our neighbor across the street also loved playing pool, and he and Dad had a great friendship until, in response to the beef crisis of 1972, the neighbor stole a refrigerated truck full of expensive beef. He got caught and went away to prison. It broke Dad's heart that his friend ended up being not a good guy.

There was also a dart board in the family room (our converted garage). Playing darts with my kids was one of the things Dad enjoyed doing when we visited.

Our parents encouraged us, got stern with us when necessary, kept us fed and clothed and occupied. We were taught how to garden, how to vacuum, how to clean the bathrooms, how to dust, and how to do laundry. We took turns making side dishes and salads, set the table and cleaned the kitchen after meals. Our parents loved us, unconditionally. That sort of upbringing, I have found, isn't normal . . . a lot of my friends around my age (and younger) have horror stories about their childhoods.

The way I was raised has given me so many gifts. I trust, probably way too easily. I see things through a happy lens, when that is not perhaps always the best way to see. For the longest time I felt I couldn't write romance novels because I didn't like conflict. I still don't but I have learned that conflict in fiction comes in many forms, and my form doesn't have to be based on anger between the hero and the heroine. This realization helped me immensely as a writer.

We had a daddy who wrote books and car columns and spent his days hustling for contracts for both, and a mom who kept house, baked cookies, worked with her husband, and told bedtime stories. We saw her take singing lessons (I spent lots of time with her at her lessons when I was very young), saw her practicing the piano, and reading novels, and saw her working with Dad, editing his work. She gardened (she loved her roses), cooked, and cleaned. My parents were a team, and even though we never saw many public displays of physical affection, the love and respect shining in their eyes for each other were palpable. Everyone who saw them saw that love.

Dad's love, outside of Mom, us kids, and his writing, was his garden, being true to his farmer roots. In the early days, we had a Meyer lemon tree and an apricot tree, and from those we learned how to stew apricots, make apricot jam, and make triple lemon cake and lemon bars. He gave away lots of apricots and lemons. I can't count how many Meyer lemon trees I have bought, and have managed to kill, since we bought our house in 1995. I think . . . finally . . . I may have a couple that will live, including a baby tree started from seed from my father's tree. Fingers crossed, as that baby tree is now about eleven inches high.

Dad grew cucumbers and made bread and butter sweet pickles. He grew tomatoes and ate them straight from the plant, still warm from the sun. He grew zucchini, bell peppers, and sunflowers and, in his later years, planted an almond tree. (He was philosophical about whether or not he'd still be around when that tree bore fruit; turns out he died before the tree had almonds on it.)

In the '70s, Dad added an apple tree, had boysenberry bushes for a long time, and never stopped growing tomatoes. Not long after we'd all left home, he started growing giant pumpkins, and planted giant sunflowers, corn, and zucchini in one section of his backyard, along with his tomatoes and onions and garlic and chives (oh, his chives!). Over time, he added a pear tree, a couple of orange trees, another apple tree, as well as a grapefruit tree that grew huge, easily twenty-five feet tall.

Dad was the one that did the stewing, the canning, the slicing, and freezing of the apples so there would be fresh apple pie in the winter. Mom had difficulties standing for long periods of time, so anything other than a standard dinner or baking activities was generally left to Dad to handle.

Every time Tom and I came to visit, the first thing Dad and I would do would be to take a tour of the garden. It was our private time, where he could update me on Mom and Scott and his writing and everything. He'd tell me his high points, his worry points, and to this day when I go outside and walk in my garden, I see Dad there, and talk to him, tell him about my day.

Dad would load me up with apples, or lemons, or grapefruit, or tomatoes, or onions . . . whatever was in season that he had way too much of would end up coming home with us. He would also load Scott up with whatever he had way too much of, which Scott counted on during the lean months.

In later years, the back half of his backyard was a maze of tomato plants over five feet tall, pumpkin plants that spread across the yard, bell peppers, corn, tall sunflowers, zucchini . . . it was magical.

Mom stopped driving in 1976, when I was sixteen. Her poor eyesight and slow reflexes, in part due to her MS, made driving hazardous, and that third accident in less than a year (and less than a block from our house) was the sign.

When all us kids had flown the nest, Dad would take Mom to writers' meetings with him. They'd go grocery shopping together. He'd take her to conferences with him. He took her to London, on cruises, to Hawaii, and to Western Writers of America conferences. Wherever Chet went, Rosie was sure to be with him in their later years. Everyone, without fail, would mention to me how much Chet loved his wife, and how Rosie was such a sweetheart with a bright smile. Everyone saw how important she was to him, and how much they loved each other. Everyone knew their names and would stop to say hello and talk to them.

There is an article out on the interwebs somewhere, that I wrote in the mid-1990s I believe, where I talk about being a part of the Sandwich Generation, caught between aging parents and children under ten. This was about the time when my dad started every discussion with me with the phrase "If I get hit by a bus . . ." and it always ended with him asking me to take care of my mother.

Rosie dying after Chet was his personal nightmare, as she was unable to live alone. He counted on me taking care of her, and I assured him that Tom and I would do so. As it turned out, she ended up dying in 2007, almost ten years to the day before he passed away.

CHAPTER THREE

Time Passages

SCOTT'S WALLET

His wallet is ocean blue, with palm trees and a sailboat and Hawaii printed on it. Still stuffed with his driver's license, his Social Security card (did no one tell him not to carry it?), business cards, credit card, the business card of the Visiting Nurse Association.

The first time I saw it when it wasn't in his possession, I found it in Dad's desk after he passed away, as we cleaned out his house in the spring of 2017. At the time, I just tucked it away into a box which I then took home, there being no room for more tears at that point. It took me eighteen months to go through those boxes (I had six boxes, Greg about three times that amount), and I threshed them down to three. The wallet stayed in the box.

The third time I saw it, I had been sad all day, so fucking sad, and it wasn't until I stirred myself to do some research for this book that I delved into the boxes again—and found Scott's wallet.

Blue. Palm trees. Sailboat. Hawaii. Scott's wallet. Such a small thing to stir up such grief. I had been grieving all day and hadn't recognized it until I held his wallet.

It's now in a drawer in my desk. Like my dad, I can't bring myself to destroy anything inside that wallet, even though I probably should.

I just can't.

Just like I can't delete my father's phone numbers from my cell phone. That means their death is reality, that I can never call, that I can never return the wallet. And while I know this to be true, my heart rebels and says, simply, no.

Many people have spoken about grief. Many words have been written about grief. To me, it's like walking on the damp sand on the beach and you don't know when the waves will rise up and crash against you, rise up over your head, swamping all your senses; or when the tide will pull back, the water receding, so your feet walk across hard, damp sand for a bit and you breathe freely, the pain a memory until the tide turns once more. When the water is above your head, it's impossible to know which way is up. You hold your breath and tread frantically, your feet seemingly far away from solid ground, the water pressing down on you until you just want to give up.

Then the tide recedes and you're gasping for air, the sun shining down. You're soaking wet with grief and yet it moves away, allows you to breathe. To settle. Sometimes for days, sometimes for months. Then years pass. You forget how it is, until a song plays, or you catch sight of the gnarled hands of an old man, or see the curve of a woman's cheek, or catch the scent of incense or star jasmine and it reminds you . . . and the tide rises again.

This is what it is to love.

Grief is something no one can get a handle on, until it happens to them. Even then, it is elusive, coming when you least expect it and rarely when everyone thinks it "should." There are a lot of folks who don't cry at funerals of their loved ones. There are also a lot of folks who cry at funerals of other people's loved ones. Sometimes, I think that's because those close to the dead are numb, and we, who are not so tightly connected, can perhaps more freely grieve for them.

Love demands grief. Grief is the gift of having loved deeply, and then lost. The two are entwined, and at some point, grief, I hope, mellows into something more sweet than bitter. But I'm not there yet.

Even after all these years—I'm not there yet.

THE CABIN: 1966—1976

In the autumn of 1966, my parents did something astonishing, and I'm still not sure how they managed to afford it. Perhaps it was the porn novels Dad had sold? At any rate, they purchased a cabin up in the Laguna Mountains, which lie east of San Diego on the eastern edge of the Cleveland National Forest. Our cabin sat about 6,200 feet above sea level, and the mountains were blanketed in Jeffrey pine trees.

Now, because it was on government-owned land (Cleveland National Forest), they could own the cabin—but not the land. They

At the cabin, maybe 1974.

actually leased the land for ninety-nine years. (That lease went with the sale of the cabin itself, renewed with the new owner for another ninety-nine years.)

It was a magical place for all of us.

We had electricity, but the hot water heater and the cooking were gas-derived, so Dad learned how to take the large, empty gas tank (it barely fit into our Ford station wagon with the seats down) into town and exchange it for a full one. Mom re-learned how to cook with gas, after having gotten used to an electric stove in the house.

There was an outhouse that we used, until Dad got a plumber up a couple years later to finish off the bathroom plumbing. The bathroom had been added on to the original octagonal cabin, about the same time as the kitchen and the sleeping porch, well before we bought it; but the plumbing for the bathroom had never been completed.

The fireplace in the center of the octagon was huge, built of what looked like rocks from the mountains all around us. My guess is the fireplace was about eight feet in diameter, a circular rock structure centered smack dab in the middle of the octagon. It had been double-sided, but at some point, the previous owner rock-walled in the side near the kitchen.

There was no heater. The fireplace was it.

The sleeping porch was on the opposite side of the kitchen structure. It had a staircase leading up to it from the outside. The windows on the sleeping porch were merely screen, which were closed in with frames covered with a heavy-duty waterproof fabric that we had to fasten in whenever we left. The windows in the main cabin had glass, but they also had hefty coverings on the outside.

In winter, those screens for the sleeping porch rarely came off. There was no electricity back there when we first bought the cabin. That was something Dad added, but that was light only, not heat. As the porch circled around three sides of the octagon, there were two double beds on either end, with an open passageway between the two, which was about four or maybe five feet wide, which is where the door to the outside was situated. Those double beds had several blankets on them, which we piled on top of our sleeping bags during winter.

At some point, Dad framed in each bedroom, providing privacy for couples. I believe he did this after Greg got married in 1973.

One of the first things Daddy did back in 1966, once the cabin was ours, was add a rope swing to the tall oak tree, slightly up the hill from the cabin. The tree was so tall that a mere ladder wouldn't be high enough to get the rope properly situated. He leaned a ladder against the tree, then from that six-foot height climbed the tree and inched out onto the limb to fasten the rope. He was thirty-eight at the time, and in great shape.

If you turned just the right way, you could swing high enough backwards to push off the roof of the outhouse. If, that is, your legs were long enough. My legs, alas, never were long enough; plus it was a tricky angle.

That first year, we were there in the snow. Snow! Daddy wrapped our feet in plastic bread bags (we used to buy bread from the Hostess Bread store, which sold goods that were out of date, making them less expensive than at the grocery store), and we had a great time. It wasn't easy getting everything to work inside, but eventually we had hot cocoa and life was so good. It was too cold to sleep out on the sleeping porch, but there were two couches that opened into beds in front of the fireplace and room for an army cot in between (which is where I slept, of course).

We spent New Year's Eve there in 1968. There was lots of snow, lots of cocoa, lots of s'mores. We still didn't have really good boots, but we had plenty of firewood to dry off chilly toes.

We ate beef stew and spent most of the evening playing games. Probe and Stratego, Hearts and five-card draw, plus game after game of Solitaire. There were probably eight decks of cards that we inherited when we bought the cabin, along with all the kitchenware. We laughed and squabbled and stretched our legs between games. We ate junk food and drank soda (not an everyday item in our house) and used the outhouse when necessary.

At midnight, after blowing our horns and dancing around like crazy kids, we bundled up and went outside. None of our neighbors were in residence, so ours were the only lights on for miles. The Jeffrey pine trees were tall and black in the moonless night, their vanilla scent lacing the air; it was so quiet and peaceful, the snow a blanket of white. When we looked up, the sky was an ocean of stars.

Pure black velvet spangled with hundreds of stars, so crowded it took my breath away. It almost didn't look real to see that many stars up in the sky. Dad pointed out the Big Dipper and the Little Dipper and promised to get a book on astronomy so we could figure out what we were seeing.

Scott sat on a tree stump and just stared overhead for the longest time. If Mom hadn't noticed him shivering, he would have stayed outdoors for hours, just mesmerized.

Our family vacations were always camping trips, which we took every other summer until Greg got married. They were filled with streams and oceans, mountains and deserts, and every single night, a campfire. In hindsight, that background instilled a love of Nature into us all. To this day, both Greg and I can feel ourselves relaxing when up among the pine trees. Whether those trees are in the Laguna Mountains or above Tehachapi or at Mammoth Lakes, that scent is in our DNA. It speaks to us as much as the sight of a sky filled to bursting with stars, or the boom and scent of the ocean.

During our time at the cabin, Scott learned the names of wildflowers and trees. He collected rocks and feathers. Whenever we were at the beach, he collected sea glass and seashells. One summer, I remember he and Dad collected a few hermit crabs, enough sea water and sand to keep them alive in a small fish tank that we had.

Alas, the poor hermit crabs didn't survive much more than a week.

When Scott was ten, his sea glass and shell collection grew to the point where Dad made him a wooden box with small shelves, padded with flat quilting fluff, to hold them. There were probably twelve to fifteen sliding shelves, and it stood a bit higher than your typical two-drawer file cabinet. At some point, the box, the shells, and the fluff all went away. I have no memory of when.

In looking back at his life, I want to say the cabin—and the experiences we had there—was his greatest outside influence; and it may well be. But then I remember he was three when Dad took the family cross-country, from Michigan to California, and I know that it was most likely that trip, at such an impressionable age, that ramped up his curiosity, that gave him a thirst for knowledge. The cabin, I'm sure, just added to what had already been stirred inside him.

We had church choir day retreats there. We had Dad's writer's retreats there. We had Methodist Youth Fellowship retreats there, where

Vacation in Canada, 1967.

the older kids teased the younger kids about snipes, those fantastical scary creatures that don't exist, and took us snipe hunting in the dark. I got to stay in the main house, but many tents and campers were on the property during these big group events.

One year, our dog Honey, a golden cocker spaniel, had seven puppies in late spring. In the summer, we took them up with us in one box . . . and brought them back, two weeks later, in two boxes, because the puppies had grown so much.

From 1966 to 1976, that cabin held our hearts, our healing, and all our hopes and dreams.

◊◊◊

The walk to the Mount Laguna General Store was a little over a mile. My parents let us walk alone, the three of us. My guess is because it gave them some time to themselves, nudge nudge, wink wink. ("A nod is as good as a wink to a blind man!" Sorry for the . . . no, I'm not. *Monty Python* for the win.)

They'd give us a couple of dollars each, and we'd go into town to the general store. Pore over the candy, crackers, and cookie selection, and then we'd walk back, our paper bags rattling nicely with each step we took. The air smelled of dust and pine trees, and it was like we were the only people in the world, as it was rare for a car to pass us once we were on the side roads to the cabin.

When it rained in the summer, and it frequently did, the rain was usually accompanied by thunder and lightning. I remember one year, Greg was on one bed on the sleeping porch usually strumming his guitar; I was in the middle on a cot, reading; and Scott was on the other bed, most likely also reading. This was before Daddy walled in the bedrooms. Our paper bags of goodies were right there with us.

At any rate, we were reading, and munching, and talking, on and off. And then this exchange happened.

Greg: Do you sometimes say "what" even when you understand what the other person said?

Scott: What?

Cue laughter as the thunder rolled and the rain came sheeting down. There is nothing like a mountain thunderstorm and laughing and being cozy with your siblings.

Greg and Scott always seemed to get along. They shared a bedroom until Greg turned sixteen, and then Dad created a room for Greg out of a portion of the family room. They never seemed to fight. Squabble, sure, we all squabbled. But bitter fights? No.

For the most part, we all got along. Greg was the Big Brother. He'd help, hinder, or ignore, as big brothers tend to do.

◊◊◊

Daddy would take us, and any guests we had, hiking all over the hills behind the cabin. We found places where the Native Americans in the area would grind up acorns, plentiful from all the oak trees around. We found deep hollows called *morteros* in big rocks, usually near those huge oak trees. We rarely, very rarely, found the rounded rocks they used to grind the acorns.

We did find arrowheads on our hikes. The Native American tribe that lived in the Lagunas was called the Kumeyaay.

Mom didn't hike with us, because even in 1966 she was unsteady on her feet, so we brought flowers and fascinating rocks back to her. One time, when it was just the three of us kids, we went to the marshy area up and over the hill, and down to the right quite a long way into a huge meadow. I have no idea how far we walked.

I was eight, I think. Scott would have been twelve, and Greg fourteen. We went down into the meadow by the marshy part. The flowers were gorgeous, and everywhere, so magical. I picked flowers, and Greg and Scott found baby frogs.

Scott always knew where the cabin was. In later years when we went, he and I would hike together. He'd collect rocks, pick flowers for Mom, and he always, always knew how to find the cabin again. If I had been out there by myself, I'd have been lost for days.

I remember one such hike. Summer, 1973; Scott would have been seventeen. It was just the four of us at the cabin that week, as about that time Greg was spending a lot of time with his girlfriend. They had recently become engaged, and their wedding was that December, so there was a lot of planning to do. He didn't go on as many family trips as he used to.

It was hot, mid-eighties; not too normal for the altitude at 6,200 feet, but at least there was a breeze. The blue jays were out, jabbering away. A woodpecker gave his signature rat-a-tat-tat-tat. I'd finished reading one of the books I'd brought with me (my packing generally consisted of books first, clothes second), and when Scott said he was going on a hike, I invited myself along.

We went up Swing Tree Hill, past the now unused outhouse, and up past the other big oak tree at the tippy top of the hill. He held the barbed wire fence open for me (when there were four strands of barbed wire, your foot went down on two, and carefully you'd hold up the other two) and I ducked through it; then I held it open for him. We hadn't gone far down the hill, heading to the right and the meadow, when the wind died.

Scott put his hand out and made me stop. He waited, and that's when I realized all the birds had stopped chirping. The mountain was silent, still, waiting.

I opened my mouth, but he shook his head, and something about the way he looked made fear crawl down my spine.

He turned back around, grabbed my hand, and we ran for the barbed wire fence. My heart was beating so hard. It wasn't until we were almost back at the cabin, the tree swing in sight, that the breeze and the forest sounds came back. We slowed to a walk.

Later, I asked him what he thought it was about, the silence, the stillness.

He shivered and didn't answer me. But I noticed that he kept watch on Mom the rest of the weekend, as if worried that something was going to happen to her. Nothing did, however, and we all made it home from that trip hale and healthy.

Cunningham's Key

By James Divine

A warm breeze blows across my face, betraying any hope that the cool morning would persist past eight AM. Summers in the Sonoran Desert are brutally hot; not that I would know any differently, being a native of Southern Arizona. I had found a spot about a half-mile from my home in the desert expanse that continued uninterrupted for hundreds of square miles into the Tucson Mountains. There were special places I had discovered in these foothills, some I could only sometimes find, even though I had carefully mapped them in my mind many times. This particular morning, I am standing in the shade of a deep arroyo surrounded by steep banks topped by scruffy Palo Verde trees and aromatic Creosote bushes. I draw patterns in the sandy riverbed with a wooden rib from a Saguaro cactus. I have nothing to guide me except memories of the Indigenous cliff drawings from a preserve further up the canyon and mandalas I had seen in an encyclopedia. I have no cell phone reception. I have no cell phone. There are no cell phones. There is no internet. I am only nine years old, and the year is 1982. I am following a deep and persistent yearning to connect with the awe of nature, which is sometimes at odds with the teachings of my Catholic upbringing. Yet here I am, intuitively drawing patterns, standing in their center, and feeling the power of the earth.

It would be almost twenty years before I discovered I was not alone in this feeling. In the autumn of 1999, a world away from the desert, I was living in the lush, green wonder of Seattle. I had been casually circling with my boyfriend's coven for over a year when they announced that they would be teaching "The Class," an experiential course on learning witchcraft. If one was deemed worthy, a student could potentially join the group. After careful consideration, I applied for entry, was interviewed by the members of the coven, and was accepted as a student. As part of the class, we were given a list of books that were "required reading." One of these was *Earth Power* by Scott Cunningham.

I had tried to read a couple of books on the Craft during the first year of dating my boyfriend, who happened to be the High Priest of his coven, the Sylvan Grove. Whether too spooky or too academic, none of the books that I borrowed from him resonated with me at that time. It was during the Sylvan Grove class when I first read *Earth Power* that a whole new realization opened for me. Before reading this book, I assumed that I could become a witch someday after achieving some sort of proper initiation and training, or perhaps when I performed a great summoning spell of some kind. After reading *Earth Power,* I realized I had been a witch my whole life.

From my childhood in the Sonoran Desert, drawing patterns in the sandy basin of the arroyos and imagining celestial power descending upon me when I sat in the center of that mandala, to the beach art I would create with my best friend in the Seattle summers between college years, I realized I was always doing witchcraft. I realized that magic is in the earth itself, and humans channel it and can do so with intention. I learned that witchcraft isn't supernatural; instead, witchcraft is *super natural*, as in extremely natural.

Today, my boyfriend, now husband, BlackCat and I are the leaders of our own coven, carrying on the legacy of our teachers and mentors. We hold them in high esteem, both the ones we knew in person, like the late, great Lady Sylvana Silverwitch, High Priestess of the Sylvan Grove; and the ones we only knew and learned from in books, like Scott Cunningham.

But Scott's legacy is not born out of knowing him personally or even knowing much about the detailed facts of his life. Scott's legacy comes from how his books created many doors people could open to access the Craft. For me, the way *Earth Power* was written made a potentially spooky thing like "witchcraft" become a beautiful practice of honoring the power and divinity of nature.

While writing this piece, I asked other witches of all generations about their experiences with Scott Cunningham. The answers I received reflected what we see from the popularity of his books. For many, witchcraft was made accessible to the individual with *Wicca: A Guide for the Solitary Practitioner*, offering one of the first books in plain language to lay out rituals, spells, correspondences, and techniques. Scott opened the doors of imagination with his reference books, especially *Cunningham's Encyclopedia of Magical Herbs*. This was a groundbreaking book at the time, and one of the first mainstream sources of magical information, especially at a time before the internet. These books, along with the many others he wrote over his lifetime, are foundational to modern witchcraft.

Besides his writing, other aspects of Scott's life and legacy are significant but far less known and certainly not officially acknowledged. Even at the time of this writing, in 2022, nearly thirty years after his death, it is still considered a "well-known secret" that Scott was gay and died of AIDS-related illness. As of this writing and before the publication of Christine Cunningham Ashworth's book, I am unaware of any official source that acknowledges these facts, nor is it mentioned in any of Scott's books. This makes sense, however, when you consider that at the time of his death in the early 1990s, being a public figure and being out as gay were very tricky, especially if one was successful. It could most certainly put success at risk. Wicca had many standards at the time for male and female fertility symbolism, and though there were many welcoming groups, anti-gay bias and heteronormative ideas were rampant. (They still are!)

All the people I knew who died from AIDS-related illness had a fair amount of shame tied up in their diagnosis and death. For the people that I knew who died early in the AIDS crisis, it was not something that was listed as a cause of death because of this shame. I can only imagine these same sentiments must have been present in 1993 at the time of Scott's death for him and his family.

As a gay-identified witch with a religious practice rooted in activism and awareness, I consider Scott to be one of our queer spiritual elders. I remember the Reagan era and the fight for funding for AIDS research. I remember joining ACT UP (AIDS Coalition to Unleash Power) in protest on the campus of the University of Arizona in 1991 and wondering if I would get arrested by the police or shot by the counter-protesters. I remember being so scared that I was sometimes ashamed and silenced from speaking up more.

In rituals, when we honor our LGBTQIA+ elders and beloved dead, we are proud to include Scott's name as a key figure in our queer ancestry, and I encourage you to do the same.

Scott Cunningham's work has impacted millions of people who have read his books and been inspired by his words. Many have gone on to start covens, write books in response, and do magic with his guidance. Today, thirty years after Scott's death, our society is very different and much the same. We live in a time when the visibility of queer, trans, and gender expression has never been more open. We live in a time when the visibility of witchcraft and information about paganism have never been more accessible. Yet we also live in a time when a powerful minority that would suppress, silence, and return us to the oppressive past has reared its ugly head.

When we give public visibility to our queer witch forbearers, honoring their successes as well as their struggles, we humanize them and offer an example and a narrative for all of us. This is especially true for the queer-identified witches of today, who can look back and see themselves as having always been represented, even if they have not always been able to be visible.

In the decades since that first training in the Sylvan Grove Class, I have become a fourth-degree High Priest in the Sylvan Tradition. That is not what makes me a witch. Being a witch is not about how many letters, initiations, memberships, books read or written one has. Being a witch is based on what witches do.

I still hold that key idea gleaned from Scott Cunningham in my heart—I am a witch because of the way I look to the natural world for the truths about the human condition and the way I channel the energies of my body and nature with my Will, feeling the power of the earth.

JUNE, 1992

After our lunch date in January, we next met at Easter at Mom and Dad's house. It wasn't noteworthy other than I made Dad's favorite, peas and potatoes in cheese sauce. That was memorable because Mom kept reminding me to add the dry mustard to the cheese sauce, even after I had done so and told her. It was my first hint that Mom had some memory issues.

I didn't see Scott again until June of 1992, for his birthday, celebrated at our parents' house. We made the trek from Los Angeles and by the time we got there, everyone else was outside on the patio, where Dad was manning the barbecue for hamburgers. The house was cool and dark, the air conditioner on in the living room and another one on in the kitchen, as it was hot, upper nineties outside, and heat and my mother did not get along due to her MS.

I remember going out to see everyone. My son, Chet, named for our father, was going on two, and a bit of a handful. When I saw Scott, I hugged him, wished him a happy birthday, then excused myself to go to the kitchen. There, behind closed doors, I cried and knew he was a dead man walking. My husband followed me and held me until I could compose myself.

Scott was thin, his face mostly bone. His eyes had begun to sink into their sockets, his skin had changed color from disease. But he held his head high, he had a smile for everyone, and my son stood at his knee and babbled freely. My father, the family photographer, had everyone gather together and took several photos with Scott holding his birthday cake and giving the camera a wry smile. Every detail of those photos is etched into my heart.

At one point during this visit, after lunch and birthday cake, Scott was in the living room on the couch. Tom and the baby and Dad and I were in there chatting with him. Somehow, we got onto the subject of contracting AIDS, how it's difficult to do, that you can't get it while hugging an AIDS patient, for instance. Not sure why we were having that conversation just then. At any rate, Dad said something about exchanging fluids.

Scott said, yeah, it all began with fluids, and we could see he was laughing about it. Tom and I laughed too, but Dad just glared. He was so angry at Scott's illness, so very angry that he was losing his son.

Mom, by the way, never knew he had AIDS. She never knew that he was gay, or if she knew never mentioned it. She knew he was extremely ill, and that his friends were concerned, but she thought he'd get better. She had her happy little bubble, and Dad let her keep it.

Correction. We all let her keep it.

The next time we all gathered was for Thanksgiving in 1992, at Greg's house in San Diego. Scott's vision was okay, and he did well with all of us, and sat for the obligatory family photo pre-feast, but after dinner he was tired and took a nap on the sofa. Mom was still ambulatory at that time, and I had a toddler, so there weren't any awkward pauses.

Tom and Scott spent some time bantering, we all talked gardening, and Scott tucked into the pecan pie, but soon after that the party broke up and we all went our separate ways.

The last Christmas we spent with him and my parents, in 1991, Scott gave me a 375 ml bottle of Veuve Clicquot champagne. I don't remember what anyone else gave me, but I will always remember that gift. He knew my fondness for the bubbles, and I'd never had real French champagne before. Mostly because I couldn't afford it. He said to me that every now and then life calls for a little bit of luxury. I've never forgotten that.

I say the "last" Christmas, because in 1992, I did not press to join the family for the holidays. I admit it. I didn't want to look at the brother I loved who was dying in a horrible way, and so I used his ill health as a reason not to spend Christmas with them. Of course, we also had a toddler, and Scott was sleeping in my old bedroom, so . . . there

Thanksgiving, 1992.

were those and other considerations, but in my heart, I know it was me being scared of seeing him so sick.

But sometimes not taking action because of fear can be what is needed. I believe now that my parents needed that quiet time with him. I believe he needed to just rest, and my family's presence would not necessarily have been very restful. Or maybe I'm just rationalizing to make myself feel better.

My presents to him at that time were ill-suited, because I didn't realize how devastated his health was by Christmas 1992. I sent a crystal to hang in the window, so he could see the flash of sunlight send rainbows across the room. I sent him other visually oriented gifts. Unfortunately, by this time, his vision was almost totally gone.

As documented in *Whispers of the Moon*, Scott's biography,

> December 15, 1992. Braving 20-degree weather, Scott Cunningham arrived in St. Paul, Minnesota, for Carl and Sandra Weschke's annual Yule party for Llewellyn Worldwide. . . . There he was, in wintertime Minnesota, barely out of a hospital bed, to say goodbye. Though tenaciously fighting his illnesses, and still writing, everyone was aware that this would probably be the last time he visited. He greeted his many friends, and, as usual, he joked.

I had no idea he went to Minnesota in the dead of winter. I'm sure the parents weren't happy about it. But in retrospect, it doesn't surprise me.

He held a deep loyalty to Llewellyn, to Carl and Sandra Weschke, and they held him in high esteem.

CHAPTER FOUR

Travels and Plants

THE EPIC VACATION

In the winter/spring of 1969, Dad decided we were going to take a long vacation. Six weeks, traveling around the country. After all, Dad could write anywhere. Greg, at fifteen, would soon not want to go on family vacations. Scott was thirteen and I was nine. Many nights during that time were spent with all five of us poring over maps of the country and talking about the best way to see the most states.

Then school was out. Dad rented a trailer to hook up to his 1968 red Ford station wagon (with the rear-facing seat!). The day before we were to set out, we kids were given a couple of dollars each and we went to TG&Y for penny candy to amuse us on the trip. Greg, Scott, and I walked together to the store, and spent our dollars well but not necessarily wisely.

The next day there was some fussing, as whoever had the rear-facing seat had the most room, but mostly the three of us were in the back seat of the car. Dad, when he bought the station wagon in 1967, paid a couple hundred dollars extra to have seatbelts installed for all five of us. Which meant whoever was in the middle in the back seat (usually me) was abnormally confined, which is why all three of us fussed to have time in the rear-facing seat. As I was the smallest, I usually got to sit there, but not always.

Finally, it was time to embark on the Epic Vacation. Going east from San Diego, we went through Arizona, stopping there for the night in the desert somewhere; the desert smelled clean, warm, of sand and sage and citrus, hot and dry. As usual, when it got dark and the fire was low, Dad would point out the constellations in the sky. It was the next morning, at our campground in Arizona, that Dad made his now-infamous fried pancakes.

See, he cooked all the bacon, and it left a lot of grease in the pan, so he used the same pan to cook the pancakes, which ended up crispy fried. My memory of this is vague, but Greg mentioned it to me recently, so I had to include it. But this might be why, most of the rest of the trip, whenever Dad cooked breakfast, instead of bacon we had Spam. It's also easier to store a can of Spam, as it doesn't need refrigeration. I still love the taste of Spam, especially when camping and for breakfast.

A day or so later it had been a long, boring day of driving, but we finally arrived at the KOA where we had reservations. Even though the trailer had a stove inside, Dad and Mom still did most of the cooking outside.

Once camp was set, and after we'd eaten dinner and explored, Dad would start a fire and we would all sit around it.

The flames reached high. *What do you see?* I don't know who said that, maybe Mom—but we all took turns describing what we saw.

As for smoke, where there is fire, smoke happens. Sometimes it followed me around; back in the day, Scott was often the one that the smoke loved. We'd laugh and switch places, and in a few minutes, the smoke would be, once again, in his face. Now that he's gone, the smoke usually finds me. I like to think Scott's just saying hi.

In Texas, we hit up Houston where the highlight was the NASA Space Center. Houston's scent was one of diesel and dust. At fourteen,

Scott was fascinated with space and the stars, and his fondest wish was to learn more, always more, about what was out there. At the time, he wanted to be an astronaut (because the upcoming first-ever moon landing was much in the news), but that faded as there was always more to learn about this world we lived in. The stars, he decided, could wait.

It seems in all the photos taken at NASA, we're bored or posing, but Dad's camera was always at the ready, as well as the Instamatic he'd bought for Mom, so we knew we were targets.

My fondest memory of Texas was at the KOA campground where we spent the night. I don't remember where we stayed, but it was green and cooler than Houston. Greg had done some scouting while scavenging firewood and met a pretty blonde teen who had been there a few nights. She assured him that the campground "had a really swell rec room." For some reason, when he reported this fascinating item back to the family, we all started giggling. Maybe it was Greg's dead-on copy of her accent? Not sure. But this memory was brought up at family gatherings for several years, often with Scott saying, "but is there a really swell rec room?"

I forgot to mention this earlier, but every state we went to, we purchased a decal for that state (and sometimes, more than one). We all got to choose, in turn, and of course Mom always got to choose, too. The far back side windows, by the time we got home, were covered in decals.

We stopped in New Orleans, but as I was only nine, and it was summertime, I did not get the full New Orleans experience. New Orleans smelled of water and decaying leaves, coffee and pastries. Dad drove us through the old neighborhoods so we could see the big plantation houses. Scott was enthralled with the trees dripping with Spanish moss, a fascination that stuck with him. We all adored beignets. We experienced everything with wide, wondering eyes. Well, that was true of most of the trip.

After New Orleans, we drove straight through Mississippi and Alabama and down into Florida. I'm sure we stayed overnight in either Mississippi or Alabama. Not much happened there, but we did stop off at a Stuckey's.

Florida smelled of sunscreen and the ocean. We ended up in Sarasota, which I remember for two reasons. First, due to all the swimming pools I'd been in during the past couple of weeks, I had a raging ear infection, my first and only, which demanded a doctor visit. And second, we went to a beach with the silkiest white sand, and the water was warm, and we were all enjoying every second of it until it started to rain, and my parents decided we needed to get out of the rain. I'm still not clear on the logic of that, especially since we ran across some sort of patch of weeds that had stickers hiding in them. Dad ended up carrying me.

It took a long time for me to forgive Florida for the pain. I was the only one to get stickers in my feet. Of course.

The next leg of our journey took us through Georgia, the Carolinas, and into Virginia. I'm pretty sure Dad snuck in history lessons during our tour of the Deep South, but battlefields didn't leave much of an impression on me. We stopped in Washington D.C. and went to the National Museum of Natural History and from a distance, we saw the White House.

The next place I remember vividly is New York City. We actually got a hotel there and found—though I'm not sure how—parking for both the car and the camper. New York smelled of cars and humanity and pizza. We took a cab to Dad's publisher (I don't remember which one at this point), and while we walked the city for a bit, Dad met with his editor and came back with books for all three of us kids and a couple for Mom, as well. As I was a champ at reading in the car, this was manna for me.

My strongest memory of New York City was in a yellow cab. I was sitting behind the driver, Dad and Scott in the front seat, Greg, Mom and I in the back seat. A stranger crossed the street in the middle of traffic, opened my door, and attempted to get into the cab with us. The cabbie yelled at him and whoever was sitting next to me yanked the door closed and pushed down the lock. Though I've been in New York City three times since then, I've never taken another cab.

Food-wise, the street pizza in New York City was the absolute best. I'd never had pizza like that, thin, so tasty, with one slice bigger than both my hands. Dad showed me how to fold it so I could eat it, and we walked and ate and took in the sights.

Scott loved and hated New York at the time. The energy, the heat, the rushing population on the streets was nothing we grew up with, and up to that point it was also nothing we'd experienced before on our travels. I believe he loved the energy and hated the lack of Nature in the city. Of course, we never did get to walk around Central Park, so maybe that had something to do with his equivocation.

Dad showed us Columbia University where he received his master's degree in journalism, and he showed us a dirty and bewildering Times Square that smelled quite rank, and it was all rather overwhelming. We did not see any shows that summer. I take that back—we saw a movie together, *Krakatoa, East of Java*. A matinee, and it got us out of the heat for a bit. I remember absolutely nothing of that movie.

(In January 1979, I was in New York City, as a prelude to auditioning for the New Haven Ballet. I ended up loving the City, as New Yorkers call their home. The surge and fall of people in the subways, the snow that looked so pure from the fourteenth floor of my hotel but proved to be dirty and sludgy at ground level, the bagels and coffee from the corner café, it all called to my soul. If I hadn't had Tom waiting for me back in California, I might have just stayed.

Upon reflection, I need to add that the City thrilled me, excited me, and scared me to death, all at the same time. I was nineteen; my entire family lived on the West Coast. A couple years later, Tom and I did discuss moving there; but I didn't want to be so far away from family. So, we stayed in California.)

Okay, back to the Epic Vacation.

After New York, we skipped New England and headed west, to Niagara Falls. We hit a snag just before going through the tunnels of the Pennsylvania Turnpike—one of the tires on the trailer caught fire. Luckily, Dad saw it and pulled over to the shoulder a bare hundred feet before the Turnpike, in which there was no shoulder. As it was, the car was right up against the guardrail, so only the driver's side doors could be opened. Cars whizzed past us so fast on the left, and Dad made everyone stay in the car.

A firetruck came after Dad had put the fire out with the extinguisher he'd brought with us. It all took time, though, as the tire had to cool before he could change it out. The firemen stayed with us, protecting us, until we could get on the road again.

Niagara Falls was beautiful, and it was such a pleasure to stand in the mists. That was at the end of a very long day, so we found our campsite and the next day went back to explore the Falls a little more.

Then it was onward through Pennsylvania, Ohio, Indiana, Illinois—Chicago, where we compared their pizza to New York City. (We loved both, though I think Scott preferred Chicago style.) Up through Iowa to Nebraska, where we drove through Shelby, Dad's birthplace. He took us to where the Cunningham family farm had been, told us how hard it had been on Grandpa Merle to have to sell the farm (which was passed to him by his parents) the summer Dad was eight. But after five years of the weather making it impossible to grow enough food to feed the family, much less food to sell, they had to choose to either sell the farm and move, or to try one more time and go deeper into debt at the bank. That part of the visit was all rather sad. I remember Scott looking across the flatness of the land, gently waving with corn and wheat.

"All this was dust?" Scott looked up at Dad. "That's why you had to leave?"

"Yep. Oh, there might be a dried-out stand of corn here and there. Whatever the wind hadn't torn up, or the late rains hadn't spoiled, or the insects hadn't eaten. But for the most part, it was all dirt brown and dried-out yellow." Dad just looked out over the field of corn, bright green in the sunshine. "Your Grandpa Merle hated selling the farm. He cried when he had to sell his horses."

Scott slipped his hand in Dad's, and they just stood there for a bit.

After Nebraska was Wyoming, where we stopped and got a motel room instead of a campground, the fourth or maybe fifth time on that trip. On July 20, 1969, we were in an air-conditioned room, crowded on the double bed, in order to watch a landmark of that year. The landing on the moon!

We watched it, knowing we were watching history, but we kids were just as interested in the built-in pool as we were in the moon landing, because the pool was just a few steps outside our motel room door. So as soon as we'd finished watching the exciting part, we were out the door and into the pool.

From Wyoming, we veered upward to Livingston, Montana, where Dad's sister Janie and her husband Lyn lived with their kids. This was the first time I can remember getting together with our cousins. Janie and Lyn had two boys and a girl, though their daughter was older than me and we didn't really hang together. But spending a couple of days there was fun.

When we left Montana, we crossed upper Idaho to Seattle, spent some wonderful sight-seeing time there (the Space Needle, Pike Street Market), and then headed down the coast to Oregon, stopped at Tillamook where Dad bought cheddar cheese, and then we turned inland, to Forest Grove, where Dad's parents Grandma Hazel and Grandpa Merle lived. We spent a good week with them.

Forest Grove, Oregon, is the home of Pacific University, where Dad got his undergraduate degree. It's a small college town. There were no sidewalks in the section of town where my grandparents lived, and trees seemed to line every street. I remember it as being a cozy place, more rural than urban. I wasn't there long enough as an adult to ever know my way around.

Their house at that time was a white two-story A-frame type, with narrow steps and a side porch, shaded by big trees. Inside was dark wood and a cramped kitchen. I believe the boys slept in the trailer, and I slept in Grandma's sewing room upstairs. The parents slept in the guest bedroom.

Their backyard encompassed a quarter of an acre and was almost a truck garden, but as far as I know they didn't sell their produce. There was no lawn to speak of, but there were rows and rows of tomatoes, beans, onions, zucchini, cucumbers. They had potatoes and bell peppers and tall sunflowers. Corn swayed in a far corner of the garden, and one side of the property line was marked by a wild tangle of blackberry bushes that must have extended a quarter of a mile. At harvest, Grandma would spend hours canning tomatoes and beans. She'd pickle the cucumbers and bell peppers, and with all the berries, she'd make blackberry jam.

Grandma would send us out with berry boxes, and Scott, Dad, and I would pick blackberries. Sometimes we'd have them, still warm from the sun, with a bit of milk and sugar. Sometimes Grandma would bake them into a pie that we'd have as dessert that night.

Whenever we visited in the summer (about every other year or so), Grandma would make Scott a birthday cake. In 1969, it was extra special for Scott's thirteenth birthday. The top was a sandy beach with an ocean wave, plus a lot of little marzipan seashells that she made. It was a spice cake, beautiful, and very tasty. To say Scott was surprised is an understatement, but then, Scott was her boy. They spent quite a bit of time together while we were there, as they did every time we visited. I don't know what they talked about, but she would take him through the gardens and talk about what they were growing.

Hazel and Scott were quite similar. She was an observer, and having grown up on farms, tended to be earth-based out of necessity. She had a love of planting, growing, harvesting, and creating from what she harvested, and a lot of that lived in Scott.

Hazel was always doing something. Sewing, baking cookies, canning, cooking, cleaning, creating apple-head dolls. Her creativity was inspiring, and I still have much of her work around my house. One year, she made us all Gonks (her name for them) and sent them for Christmas. They were large roundish creatures, pillows really, about sixteen inches tall and twelve inches wide with pants and faces and funny, thin arms. We loved those things. Mine absorbed many a tear over the years; I still have Scott's, up on a closet shelf.

She showed Scott and me how to make corn dollies from fresh corn husks, none of which I remember, though I know Scott kept his for a long time. He learned how to make dried apple-head dolls, though I don't know if he did so when we got home.

While we were there, we had at least two big family gatherings that included our great aunts and great uncles and their kids, plus their kids' kids. When Hazel and Merle moved to Oregon in 1937, they had one distant cousin in Corvallis that they stayed with until they could rent a place. More family moved into the area after '37, but those first couple of years were lean ones.

The family gatherings that summer in 1969 were such fun. One was a potluck picnic at a local park. There were more kids that we were either directly or tangentially related to than we'd ever been around before, and we played tag and Red Rover and hide-and-seek in the park. We got to know my Uncle Kenny's daughter Lori and his step-kids in this setting.

Scott was the only one of us kids who wore glasses, so that set him apart a bit at first, but as he gave as good as he got, and could run and tumble along with the rest, any sense of separateness soon vanished.

Of course, there was an abundance of good food. Cold fried chicken, thick sandwiches, spaghetti casserole, deviled eggs, corn casserole, cold cooked green beans, hot dogs and hamburgers from the grill, homemade pickles of all types, not to mention the cakes, cookies, pies, and other sweet treats. Sodas, of course. If there was beer, I don't remember it; most of the family were Methodists.

Because it was in the eighties temperature-wise on many days while we were there, and most folks didn't have air-conditioning in their houses up in Oregon, our cousin Lori, her step-siblings, and we three would walk to the local public pool, which was quite an adventure. Greg, the oldest at fifteen, was charged with keeping us all in line. As we all got there and back again without fail, I'd say he did a good job.

Then, finally, it was time to start the last leg of our trip. Dad always found us amazing campgrounds, mostly by instinct. One such was the Arizona Beach campground in Oregon. There was the forest, then a long hike down to the beach. At the time, it seemed the best of both worlds, and all of us thoroughly enjoyed the place. We were sad at only spending one day there, but we were all getting tired of being on the road. Mom and Dad decided to make the most of the last of the trip, and so we took Pacific Coast Highway much of the way. I remember Dad stopping when he saw a man selling cold, freshly cooked crab on the side of the road. He bought two, and we found a place to pull over and we had a feast of crab and bread.

We were so ready to be home when we finally got there. I remember the drudgery of unpacking the trailer, the mounds of laundry Mom and I did. I remember Dad going to pick up the mail from the post office. Three bins full! He was quite stoked, and I believe there were some checks in there, which made going through the junk mail worthwhile.

The one constant, from state to state to state, was Stuckey's. Gas, bathrooms, snacks, meals, saltwater taffy (one of Scott's favorites), and that pecan candy that Mom so loved. I can't tell you how relieved we all were when we were hungry and saw a Stuckey's sign ahead.

Oh, and something that Greg reminded me of recently. We'd listen to the rock 'n roll radio stations as we crossed the country. When we left California, we were hearing "brand new music" hit the airwaves. As we crossed states, we heard that same "brand new music"—touted as such by each new DJ—so many times we got sick of it. Then, by the time we were on the East Coast, the music was new again until we headed to the middle of the country on the way back, and heard the same "new" songs. I guess the two coasts got new music first, before the middle of the country? I don't know.

So that's the Epic Vacation, the last vacation we all took together as a fivesome family. In looking back, I know we spent a lot of time hot and sticky and cranky in the back seat of the car, because the car didn't have air-conditioning; but sitting beside the open car window, and leaning on the locked door, the wind in my face, was absolute heaven.

There were brilliant moments: campfires; s'mores; the ocean; motel rooms; lots of built-in pools; New York City pizza (they sell pizza on the street! And the slices are huge!); and the bayous of Louisiana. We had Stuckey's, that highway beacon where we could gas up the car and get something tasty to eat, and the redwood forests, "a really swell rec room," and the man on the moon. And there were awful moments: each of us had at least one bout of "gotta stay near the bathroom for a while" during the trip; my doctor visit; feeling like if we didn't get out of the car, we'd each one of us scream ourselves deaf; and laundromats across the southern states, which were uniformly terrible places.

But it was all of a piece, and I had to dig deep for the awful moments because what remains crystal, what resonates over the years, are the brilliant moments. We were family, and as long as we were together, there wasn't anything we couldn't handle. That safety had always been a part of our life.

What Scott Cunningham Did for Herbalists Everywhere

By Amy Blackthorn

As with so many witches, Wiccans, and Pagans, discovering a copy of *Wicca: A Guide for the Solitary Practitioner* as a young witch changed my life forever. And yet there's more to be seen in Scott Cunningham's work.

As a child, I lived in an inner-city apartment with my parents and three siblings. There were few trees in our neighborhood, and our postage-stamp-sized yard had hardscrabble grass and a small patch of mint by the door to the basement. I was about five or six when I discovered the mint in the yard and asked my mother about it.

"That's peppermint," she said. "It is used to make tea, and other things, like the mint candy you enjoy." This knowledge blew my mind. As a child who had no experience with open farmland, only used to walking to the grocery store at the end of the block, it hadn't really occurred to me to ask where the groceries came from, much less where candy came from.

Fast forward a year, and we were moving to the country, where our small, one-stoplight town was named after a breed of cow, and kids at the high school rode tractors to school. Our new home had two large maples, and there were two azalea bushes along the side of the house. While examining our new flora, I brushed one of the magenta flowers. I worried I'd broken the flower when inside this tiny cup, where the flower had previously rested, I saw a tiny black seed. It was as if the universe's secrets were being revealed to me alone. Plants grew flowers, which then became seeds, to make more plants! I was hooked, and I had to know everything about plants there was to know. Pretty soon, I was doing chores for neighbors to earn money to buy a window box, a six-pack of petunias, and a bag of media from our local grocery store, peddling home on my bike with the soil thrown over the handlebars. This was my first introduction to magic; the life cycle of plants was the mystery revealed to my young mind.

I would only come upon Scott's work in another three years, thanks to an eager child's desire for inclusion in an older sister's shenanigans. As a teen, I was still so entranced by the work of plants that I attended a specialty high school where I learned about cultivating plants, running a greenhouse, and designing my hydroponic systems. Meanwhile, parallel to my horticulture work, I was studying witchcraft. When I found *Cunningham's Encyclopedia of Magical Herbs*, the link between my love of plants and the religion I was researching intersected: my heart exploded with joy and everything clicked.

For an herbalist, it can be challenging to find books that discuss the metaphysical implications of plant-based spellwork. This was especially true in the early to mid-'90s. Many had a summary table with a few esoteric-sounding plants, their mystical associations, and little expansion beyond that. With the publications of Scott's *Encyclopedia of Magical Herbs, Magical Aromatherapy,* and *The Complete Book of Incense, Oils, and Brews,* there was suddenly a vast amount of information available to coincide with the availability of more esoteric plants, as well as magical uses for things commonly found in the spice cabinet.

Scott's *Encyclopedia of Magical Herbs* is still one of the most commonly recommended magical herbals because of the breadth and depth of the information given. It includes within its pages esoteric plants, including varieties of seaweed (likely owing to a life lived by the sea), mushrooms, and plants not native to the continental United States. Prior to this, modern books had a handful of common associations for only a few botanicals that were placed on a pedestal as "the" magical plants. Now we understand that all plants have inherent spiritual properties. I work tirelessly to help people understand where the strengths of each plant lie and, more importantly, how to discern these properties for themselves. There will always be plants we are drawn to that aren't found in any magical text due to rarity, popularity, or a lack of understanding of the plant. One of the most essential things any facilitator can do is to empower their students to reach beyond the material presented, forge new paths through the forest, and reach new heights.

Each new book that Scott introduced brought countless people to the hidden realm of botanical understanding. He helped advance and preserve the witches' duty to bridge the worlds of the seen and unseen through our plant allies, whether through making incense, working with dried material, blending essential oils, or cultivating the living plant. I am honored to continue this legacy after him.

CHAPTER FIVE

Changes, So Many Changes

THE TEENAGE YEARS—1970s

I was thirteen and Scott seventeen when Greg moved out of the house after his marriage in December 1973. That year Mom became a substitute teacher for special ed classes in the San Diego School District. She had a bachelor's degree in pscyhology and had gotten her teacher's certificate in special education.

The year 1974 was tough for Scott. He was diagnosed with hepatitis A and had to keep to his room for weeks. Dad took his dinners to him on paper plates and plastic utensils, which got tossed after they'd been used. His laundry was washed on hot and all by itself. I wasn't allowed to use our bathroom; instead, I used the parents' bathroom.

We all had to get shots as a preventative measure. After he recovered, life went back to normal, and his illness was never spoken of again. During this time, and before I started going to the ballet studio after school every day, now and then Scott would knock on my door. I was either reading or, well, reading.

He always had something interesting to test out on me. One of the first things I remember was dripping candle wax into water. To make protective medallions, he said, and to divine the future. I have no idea where he got all the colored candles. These were the more expensive, full-on tapers that were all one color, not white candles dipped in a colored coating, which were easy to find and relatively inexpensive. We used cooking pots that we filled with water and took turns dripping the wax into the water in a somewhat circular shape. Color always came first, and we'd always end with either white or a dark blue as a backdrop to the rest of the wax.

When we were done, he'd lift out the medallion and flip it over, running his finger over the bumps and the colors. He'd tease me by pretending to tell me my fortune, which he inevitably ended with me cleaning up my room. (Even back then, I was more comfortable in a creative mess than I was with tidiness.)

I kept those wax medallions until they grew dusty and colorless. At first, I'd kept them because they reminded me of good times. Then I kept them because they were a link to Scott. But when I came across them again in the far recesses of a desk drawer in 2006, after forgetting about them for years, I knew it was time to let them go.

As Halloween was coming up, I saved them and ended up using them as a fire starter of a sort. It didn't really work, and I don't recommend it, but once the fire really got going, the wax did burn nicely. It was a small fire, out in our fire ring in the backyard, and as they burned, I talked to Scott while watching the fire fairies blow about. It all helped settle me as that was a particularly difficult year. While it may look like I was letting go a part of our history, I was actually creating new history for us. Now, every Samhain (or as close as I can get), I have a small fire, and I spend some time talking to my brother. It's not the only time I talk to him; but it's definitely a date I keep.

Scott also loved making candles. He would stand at Mom's electric stove and dip long wicks into tall coffee cans set in a big pot of hot water holding melted wax, patiently dipping, dipping, dipping until the wax had gathered enough mass to actually look like a taper. After his death,

I found several of these tapers, pale blue, about six inches long, uncut, two to a wick.

For years, those candles hung in the hallway to my office. Finally, I moved them from the hallway to the corkboard in my office. They've melted and gotten dusty and bulgy, but I still have them.

One night in June 1974, Scott came home from the very first Gay Pride parade ever held in San Diego, put on by the Center for Social Services, a brand new social and political focus for the gay community. He told me this story, years later, about what a great time he'd had. But it was very late, and when he got home, Dad was still up.

Apparently, Scott was still wearing his Pride buttons and it didn't take Dad more than a second to understand where he had been, as the parade had made the news and Dad never missed watching the news.

But all he said that night was that he was glad Scott got home safely. Then he turned and went to bed. Scott told me he knew then that, while his sexuality would never be an open conversation with our parents, they weren't going to kick him out of the house, and they weren't ever going to stop loving him. Being witchy and being gay wasn't easy in the '70s.

One good thing it did, however. Mom and Dad stopped talking about his dates (or lack thereof), and lifted that social pressure off him. I don't know how Dad got Mom to stop discussing it, but she did. In retrospect I can almost hear Scott's sigh of relief.

Yes, we had loving parents. They were at base conservative, but they were both college graduates. Dad had seen wartime. A basic tenet of theirs was definitely "live and let live." And I'd have to add, "be kind" was also dear to their hearts, though they never said either of those adages; rather, they embodied them.

◊◊◊

In 1968, summer I believe, Mom and Dad allowed the boys to paint their closet doors a flat black, and then to paint "graffiti" on them with poster paint that glowed under a black light. They would have been twelve and fourteen that year; two years after this, Greg moved into his own space in the converted garage that he and Dad built. It was the first step in Greg's independence, and the first real step in Scott's ability to grow in the Craft there at home.

Recently I asked Greg what year the black closet doors happened, and he replied thusly—"I don't remember doing that, statute of limitations." Of course, I can't find a photo that proves it.

◊◊◊

Greg asked me recently when I realized Scott was gay, and I had to take a moment or two to think about it. When I was young, I didn't know what being gay meant. Once I started hanging out in the ballet studio on a regular basis, and dancing with the men there, I realized there were men who loved the ladies, and men who loved the men. So, I was most likely twelve or thirteen when I realized Scott was gay. It seemed normal, because I was around it all the time. And frankly, I felt safer with the men who loved men. In that kind of environment, where there are men and teenage girls (to be fair, some of the guys were in their late teens, too) all barely covered in leotard and tights, knowing who was safe to be around and who you didn't want to be alone with was hugely important. The ballet studio is where I learned to be wary of men, to watch their behavior, and to listen to my intuition.

Scott stood about six-two, with broad shoulders. He liked Hawai'ian shirts and jeans; started losing his hair in his late twenties. His eyes were a sparkling blue behind his glasses, and he would lift an eyebrow whenever he thought I was being kinda stupid. He hated being lied to, didn't trust quickly, and would do anything for our parents.

He also did what my husband Tom calls "chorus boy dressing room banter" quite well. Tom was in numerous musicals; oftentimes, over half the men in the chorus were gay.

Scott Cunningham of the Rainbow Dead

By Storm Faerywolf

Modern witches of all stripes owe a tremendous debt to Scott Cunningham. He was the author of numerous bestselling books on magic and spirituality and was instrumental in making the religion of Wicca accessible to people outside the lineaged coven structure, much to the chagrin of many a traditionalist. His book *Wicca: A Guide for the Solitary Practitioner* changed the name of the game for many a witchcraft seeker, bringing the mysteries of the once-elusive Wicca as close as one's living room, for any who wanted to do the work.

In a time in which the practice of Witchcraft was seen as sinister by outsiders and often treated like an ego-based organized religion by hardline insiders, he made the Craft accessible to the seeker outside of the rigid coven system, harkening back to the ancient roots of our Craft as healers, midwives, cunning men, and wise women. His work was an extension of his own insatiable curiosity, leading him into many different places in which he found the hidden magic and then drew it out so that others could more easily see it for themselves.

Though I had read many books on magic and occultism in my youth, *Cunningham's Encyclopedia of Magical Herbs* was one of the very first books I found on *practical* witchcraft. A reference book, with many entries for numerous plants and flowers and steeped in a rich brew of folklore and personal experience (and not to mention some *very* handy tables of correspondences), this was the book that allowed many a would-be witch or warlock the space to experiment and form allies with our good neighbors in the plant kingdom.

At the tender age of fourteen, I would spend hours in my local library copying down the entries for selected herbs and plants in my notebook and then began my own formal practice based largely upon this and some other available works. Two years later I would feel similarly about *Cunningham's Encyclopedia of Crystal, Gem and Metal Magic*, which opened up a whole new world of geological allies in my personal work. Where most other books on the Craft stressed the need for adherence to a circle, coven, or working group (often with overly complicated rituals), Cunningham brought the core of the work to the individual and focused on the magical relationships between the practitioner and the natural world. Titles like *Earth Power* and *Earth, Air, Fire & Water* set the stage for a simple magical spirituality rooted in the natural world, one in which anyone could participate as long as they took the time to commune with Mother Earth.

His work represented a significant turning point in the modern Craft, allowing thousands of seekers an opportunity to connect to the divine hidden within nature, and themselves, and by extension, with each other through a shared worldview.

One aspect of Scott Cunningham's life that many did not know at the time of his success was that he was gay. He may not have used that particular term himself (it was not something that he was particularly open about during his life), but his family and friends knew that he had relationships with other men. He was somewhat private in relation to the larger world, never publicly stating his orientation one way or another. Public declaration or not, in 1974 he attended the very first San Diego Pride Parade and was open about himself with those with whom he was close. Though he was celibate in the last decade of his life, this should not erase the reality that he was a gay man.

For queer Crafters, this is an important bit of our collective Craft history. We, who have often taken a backseat to the heteronormative views and philosophies of many of the early Craft elders, can take pride in the fact that one of the most prolific writers and teachers of the Craft, who for many practitioners was perhaps the very first exposure they had to the modern Paganism, was a gay man. But the truth of this is not only relevant to the thousands of queer witches, warlocks, and other wonders practicing today, but also to anyone who has ever benefitted from or been exposed to Cunningham's extensive body of work, and this pretty much means everyone in the Craft. For many, he was the entry point for our magical studies, and even for those trained in a coven setting, very often those covens would also at times reference his work. To know that a gay man was so influential to the development of the modern Witchcraft movement should be a reminder that it is diversity that makes us stronger. If you are practicing any form of the Craft today, especially that outside of a tradition or coven, you have a queer person to thank for it. Hail Scott Cunningham! What is remembered lives.

1970S, CONTINUED: A CHORUS LINE

In the '70s, we had new neighbors down the street a bit, and their last name was Devine. Eva was the Devine matriarch, and she loved Scott. Her oldest daughter and Scott were in many of the same classes together, and Mom and Dad would invite people on the block to our house, so neighbors got to know each other as a matter of course.

Eva was Italian, maybe five feet tall, slender, with short black hair and dark eyes that always seemed to be laughing. All her children were taller than she was, but she ruled their home with love and a backbone of steel.

Over the years, Eva and Scott developed a dear friendship. "Eva, baby!" and "Scott, baby!" were their shout-outs whenever they saw each other. Scott would often drop by their house on the way home from school, and he and Eva would chat. I know that after he moved out, he would still drop by every now and then to check up on her.

Eva was devastated when Scott died. Years later, I saw her when I had visited Dad, and we spent a bit of time reminiscing. She loved him like a son, she told me. Too soon after that trip, Eva passed away as well. I like to think she's calling Scott "baby" now, and that they're enjoying the hell out of each other.

In Eva Devine's heart, Scott was one of her own. Just as she was one of his own. They were family, and I guess that's the first time I saw it in action . . . family made, as opposed to family born. It gave them both so much joy.

◊◊◊

One of my favorite memories with Scott during my teen years is watching *Funny Girl* with Barbra Streisand on TV. Now, it came out in the theaters in 1968, so this was probably 1972 or 1973 timeframe. He'd make popcorn and we'd sit, and laugh, and I'd try to talk and he'd shush me. At one point in the movie, you can hear giggling during a huge production number, and Scott told me that was me giggling. I must not have had much brain at that point, because I completely believed him. But then, Scott was good at leading me down harmless garden paths.

This was back in the days of three- to five-minute commercial breaks, so we'd stay riveted on the living room floor, laughing our guts out, until a commercial came on. Then race to the bathroom, or to get more popcorn, or whatnot.

Another Barbra favorite was *What's Up, Doc?* with Ryan O'Neal, which first ran in movie theaters in 1972. We saw this as a family. This film was pure Buck Henry and Peter Bogdanovich genius, and if you haven't seen it, I highly recommend it. While not a musical, per se, there is quite a bit of music in the movie.

Every year for years on Thanksgiving weekend, we watched *The Wizard of Oz*. Again, it was an event. The entire family would get together to watch it, popcorn and soda at hand. It was a comforting routine.

Scott and I watched all the musicals from the '30s and the '40s together. Another pleasure was watching *The Carol Burnett Show*. Every Saturday, like clockwork, he watched it with me . . . until he had a car, and then he was gone many weekend nights.

He also loved newer stage musicals. He borrowed the album to *Jesus Christ Superstar* from a friend, so we knew most of the lyrics before we ever saw the movie. He'd put it on the big record player in the living room, and we'd sit and look at the lyrics on the back of the album (really tiny print) and sing along. Unfortunately, we only got to keep the album for a weekend.

The double album of *Jesus Christ Superstar* came first and was released in October of 1970. In 1971, Scott went with me and a group of kids from the Methodist Youth Fellowship group to see the movie when it finally came to the screen. Parents that might not have let their kids go did so because it was under the aegis of the church. The movie had a profound resonation for both of us, though we didn't talk much about what we'd seen. I'd have been eleven, and Scott would have been fifteen. We didn't talk religion. It was just a fact in our lives. At that age, I was still going to the Methodist Church Sunday School. Scott was in the youth choir. Greg pretty much went his own way.

◊◊◊

I turned sixteen in February 1976, and my birthday present from Scott was a ticket to see *A Chorus Line* at the Shubert Theatre in Century City up in Los Angeles, later that summer.

To say I was excited would be an understatement. I was dancing at the time with California Ballet Company. I was still in the Junior Company and not yet a company dancer. I've gone through the California Ballet online history, and I'm not really there, so don't look for me, but dance was my life at that time.

One weekend day, Scott drove me up to L.A. We got there early, and he took me to Capezio's Dance Shop on Vine Street in Hollywood. I bought a beautiful green v-neck leotard with skinny straps in a silky, stretch fabric that I loved. Scott approved the color, as he said it matched my eyes. I might have picked up some pointe shoes, too, as I had been ordering mine from their store for a year or so by that point. Then we went to see the show at the Shubert.

I had performed on the San Diego Civic Theater stage, and it held more people, but being at the smaller Shubert made me feel terribly grown up. The women were for the most part dressed up. They were all heels and hose, perfume and jewelry, lipstick and on the arm of a proper companion. I was most likely in one of my church-going dresses, and Scott in church clothes, as well. But there were plenty of young dancers in the audience, so we didn't feel too out of place in our nosebleed seats.

I found the musical amazing. It caught me up in my dream of being a dancer for a living and tossed me straight into the heartaches and joys of that life. The song "Everything Was Beautiful at the Ballet" both broke my heart and gave me shivers. I was a dancer, and those people up there were like me.

The show also gave me another window into performing, outside of ballet but within the dance world. It was while watching this show that I decided yes, I wanted to dance for a living. (That didn't last long.)

On the way home that evening, we stopped at McDonald's and had dinner, and talked almost the entire way back to San Diego about the performance, the actors, the choreography. Scott had taken some dance in high school, plus he'd been in drama classes, so we could discuss what we saw on a practical level as well as an emotional one.

That Scott would think to give me this experience of *A Chorus Line* showed how thoughtful he was with his gift-giving. He always put a lot of thought and effort into his giving, and it always seemed to be something you didn't know you wanted but were absolutely delighted to have, which is a special talent. Plus, his wrapping skills were top of the line.

◊◊◊

In 1977, Scott decided he should join the military, and chose the Navy. This made sense as he could go to basic training there in San Diego at the Naval Base.

From a logistics point of view, it made sense. In every other way possible it made no sense at all. Scott was not a guns 'n ammo kind of guy. My brothers never played cowboys and Indians, or war of any kind (except the card game). He wasn't a big sports guy, player, or fan; choosing the military was so out of character for him.

I don't know if he made that choice because of a broken heart, bad relationship, feeling helpless, a past life experience, or what. At twenty, he was still living at home, and none of his jobs made him decent money; he hadn't yet started writing *Magical Herbalism* (published in 1982), so he didn't have that to anchor him. His car was a used Ford Pinto wagon in shades of blue that Dad helped him buy when Scott started at San Diego State University.

We all tried to talk him out of joining the Navy. Even though I had just passed my driver's test (finally), and I knew I'd get the use of his car while he was in Basic, I still didn't want him to go. It felt all wrong, like a too-tight suit that strangled your armpits and thighs and made walking difficult.

But he was an adult, and legally able to join up, so he did.

I don't think any of us believed he'd actually go through with it, because we were all shocked when the day came and he said goodbye to Mom and me, and Dad drove him to the naval base.

Yes, I got the car, but I was devastated. The parents could at least be proud of him continuing military service in our family, but I didn't understand, and the thought of my peace-loving brother willingly learning how to shoot a military rifle confused me.

Well before his time in basic was up, he suddenly and inexplicably was home again, with the buzziest of buzz haircuts ever. I was happy he was home, and unhappy I had to give his car back to him.

When we talked about it later, he said it felt wrong the minute he stepped on base, but he gave it a good try. When it became obvious to him he was in the wrong place, he started working magick on getting an early discharge, and then because I believe due to budget cuts, new recruits were given a chance to change their minds, and so Scott came home.

Magick works.

CHAPTER SIX

Opportunities Abound

ADULTS—ORANGE AVENUE

How did Scott and I come to live together as adults? In 1976, I had decided I needed to get out of high school as quickly as possible, mainly because I felt I didn't belong. This feeling grew after Scott took me to see *A Chorus Line*. I saw the passion for dance, for theater, there on the stage, and I knew I had the same passion.

I looked at the kids I went to school with, and they were interested in dating, and movies, and the football game. Nothing wrong with that, but I was actively working toward my future career in dance. I was at the studio six days a week by then and spending upwards of four hours a day on weekdays on the dance floor, longer on Saturdays, between classes and rehearsals. At sixteen, I felt infinitely older than just about everyone at high school. I had my small circle of friends, and I was never bullied; rather, I was ignored, and considering how many kids went to school while I was there, I was happy to blend into the background.

I worked with my school counselor to get an early graduation. It was a matter of taking an extra class or two during each of my remaining semesters, and since I wasn't going to go to college straight out of high school, they were fine with letting me have slightly longer days.

At any rate, I managed to graduate in January of 1978. Finally, I could start my life without being tied to school.

Scott had a job, and I had a job with the ballet company through a state grant, doing lecture demonstrations of ballet at the local schools. I think I was making a hundred bucks a week, or maybe a bit more. One day he approached me as I was sewing ribbons onto my pointe shoes.

"So. Chris. We both have jobs."

"Wonder of wonders. What's up?"

"It's time I moved out. Want to share an apartment? I think we can swing it, if it's not too expensive."

I just stared at him. "Move out?"

"Yeah. You'll get to spend more time with Tom, and I'll have some breathing room."

"But where will we go? I don't know anything about finding a place to live."

"We'll figure it out. You in?"

I shrugged. "Sure."

With my parents' blessing and consent, Scott found a surprisingly roomy two-bedroom apartment for us at 4349 Orange Avenue (he said the numbers were auspicious) for the amazing rate of $150 a month. A few days before my eighteenth birthday in 1978, we moved in together. (The apartment on Orange Avenue is no longer there; that building and the one next to it were sold and torn down to make way for something new.)

All the utilities were in Scott's name, mainly because I was seventeen and . . . can you even get electricity turned on in an apartment when you're seventeen? I don't think so. This was one of many details he handled while I was at the ballet studio.

My parents had been gifting us with household-type gifts for a while (a hint to get us out of the house, perhaps), so we had a card table for the kitchen table, and I believe we had an old couch of our parents'. We each had our beds and our desks, and of course we swiped what we could from Mom's kitchen, though she helped out with taking us shopping and setting us up with the basics—oil, flour, sugar, spices, Bisquick, plus pots and pans and Melmac dishes. Scott ended up doing most of the grocery shopping.

Our first meal wasn't that exciting. Spaghetti and jarred sauce, with garlic bread from the store and a salad, because Mom always had salad with our dinners. We sat in our tiny kitchen on folding chairs at a card table covered with an old beach towel and started the adventure of being adults on our own.

Thinking back, it was strange and wonderful, that moving-in period. We did it fairly fast, over a weekend. It was my first time deciding where things should go in a place I'd never been in before. Scott had lots of ideas about that, and we bickered good-naturedly about how to set up the kitchen, but for the most part it was easy.

We lived on Orange Avenue together for about eight months. I was rarely there, as I had a boyfriend by that time (my husband, Tom Ashworth—we married in 1980), and I ended up spending most of my time with Tom at his apartment because—love. (And sex, ha! No, seriously. Sex.)

Outside of the day we moved in, and a handful of other days when I'd come in to grab fresh clothes, I don't have any memories of Scott and me in that space together. No memories of shared meals except for that first one. No wondering if the other was coming home that night, as Scott knew if I wasn't there, I was with Tom and therefore safe. After the first couple of nights, I never spent a night there with Scott also being there in the evening. In fact, I think I may have spent only six or seven nights there, the entire eight months we lived together.

At eighteen, I was experiencing freedom. I was dancing under contract with California Ballet under the CETA grant, I had a place I could crash if I needed to (the Orange Avenue apartment), and I had a man I loved, so it makes sense that I wasn't around much at the apartment. I don't think I have a single photo of Scott and me there together, which makes me sad.

As I said earlier, I already knew Scott was gay. I will say this about that: Scott was an intensely private person. We never discussed our sex lives, we never discussed his relationships, past or present (if he was in one, I never knew), and we never spent much time together in social settings, unless it was with our family and family friends.

At one point, Scott took me to a gay bar (not The Brass Rail, which was the most famous one in San Diego at the time, but a different one). He decreed I should wear all black—so I wore black bell bottoms and a black button-down shirt, with a few buttons unbuttoned and no bra because I just didn't need to wear one at five foot four and about a hundred and ten pounds.

The bar was fascinating (they didn't card me, and I always wondered if it was because Scott knew the bartender), and oh, did I get compliments on my "breasts," which were slight, and how "femme" I looked—Scott laughed a lot about that on the way home. It never occurred to me that people thought I was a guy until Scott enlightened me.

But in spite of all this, there was a fear in me that I can now acknowledge. One I've regretted ever since. Our second day in our new home was a Sunday. I didn't have rehearsal for once, and Tom and I hadn't made any plans for the day, so I was still settling in, washing ballet clothes in the bathroom sink. Scott was setting up his office in his bedroom when the phone rang. Remember, this was back in the day of wired phones and answering machines.

He told me a friend was coming over, and they had books they were going to exchange, and maybe they were going to grab a pizza. I had originally planned to spend the night there at the apartment. But for some stupid knee-jerk reason, instead of staying and meeting this friend, I suddenly needed to get out of there. I grabbed clean ballet clothes and a few non-ballet clothes to take to Tom's place and left with some stupid excuse on my lips.

Why was I afraid? I don't have a clue. Maybe because I'd almost never met any of his friends, even while we were growing up? I don't know, but it still bothers me to this day that I up and ran out. I love my brother, but even though I grew up with him, I didn't know him very well. We weren't the type of people who sat around and had deep conversations about our feelings, because we weren't brought up that way. And while I had a job and a career I loved, I was barely eighteen and still quite selfish.

Now, I think, I'm ready to have those deep conversations. Now that my empathy has ratcheted up to eleven, now that I have the weight of my years behind me. But then? I was just too young.

I didn't go back for a couple weeks, other than to help pay bills and change out my clothes. I would do my laundry at Tom's place, as his apartment building had a laundromat. My room was a wreck—clothes strewn all over the place, unmade bed, an unused scent to it. Scott told me that early one morning, Dad had shown up at the apartment—not sure why—and looked into my room.

Of course, I wasn't there; just the scattered detritus of a life barely lived in that apartment. He only closed the door, and never spoke of it to either one of us.

On one level, I'm sure Scott didn't mind that I was rarely there. He had an apartment to himself, and I paid for half of rent and utilities. On another level, maybe he did mind that his sister fled meeting one of his friends to spend time with her boyfriend. I don't know. We never discussed it. And I never got the opportunity to meet any of his friends, ever again. My loss.

Let me underscore that. Not getting to meet the people who were important in his life was a major loss for me. If I had been open and welcoming to that person, whoever it was, would I have been drawn into more of Scott's life? Met more of his friends, taken to more places he cherished? I don't know. I'll never know. So when I say it was my loss, I mean it at the deepest level possible.

Another pattern in my family: Whatever is truly important is not discussed. Case in point, I didn't learn that my Uncle Kenny Cunningham, Dad's brother, a World War II veteran and POW, had died until I called Dad one day and asked, hey, how's Uncle Kenny?

Dad's response? "Oh, he died a couple months ago. Didn't I tell you?"

What I have learned within the last few years is that Scott normally didn't cross-pollinate his friends. If you were family, you didn't get to meet any of his friends. If you were one of his Wiccan friends, you didn't get to meet his high school friends (unless they were the same people). His writing friends didn't meet his Wiccan friends, and so on and so forth.

For all I know, had I stuck around that night, Scott might have met his friend on the steps outside and left without introducing me. But I doubt it.

A friend of mine once asked me if I thought Scott was private because he *was* a private person, or because he *had* to be. I had to put some thought into it, but the short answer is both. The longer answer is, he was always private. When you think about it, he was gay, and knew it at a fairly young age. That alone would ensure he kept his thoughts and feelings to himself. As he grew older, and as his interests in earth and magick and Wicca grew, he found himself in two closets, not just one. When his writings became more known, he was private in that unless you were in his inner circle, he wouldn't talk about his hopes, dreams, desires.

Scott was, however, a giving man. Later on, when his publisher forwarded fan letters to him, he answered them. When online bulletin boards became a thing, he interacted in that community, and helped out when he could. He would take phone calls from strangers who had questions or needed help in some way that he could provide. He gave his time, energy, and attention to those who sincerely needed it.

So, we shared a space. When an opportunity came up for me to audition for Arizona Ballet Theater in Phoenix in July of 1978, I talked to my parents about it, but never really discussed it with Scott. I did tell him I was going to audition, but we both knew there were no guarantees with that sort of thing.

Three or four of us from California Ballet ended up auditioning. Before I left San Diego for the audition, I went to Balboa Park where Tom was rehearsing a play for Starlight Opera and said goodbye to him. He'd given me a paper map, with the route highlighted in yellow, and hugged and kissed me. I made the ten-hour drive from San Diego to Phoenix and went to Tom's family to stay the night and rest before the audition the next day.

There I was, eighteen years old, meeting my boyfriend's parents—at midnight, after a very long car drive. The three ladies that brought Tom up—his mother, grandmother, and aunt—were lovely, warm, and welcoming. After making sure I didn't want anything to eat, they showed me to Tom's old room and let me sleep. After the audition, I drove back to San Diego that same day, with another girl from San Diego that I didn't know very well.

I got into my first-ever car accident on the way home, not even out of the city limits. My dad ended up putting us on a plane for home, and my car stayed in the lot of a full-service gas station that happened to be on the corner lot where I limped to after running a red light and plowing into a cream-colored Cadillac. Not my best moment, for sure. (And it turned out that the man who worked at the gas station that helped get us to the airport to fly home was related to one of my grandmother's best friends in Oregon. Weird, huh?)

It was just a day after I got home that I got the call—and the job! The car, however . . . Dad and I drove out to Arizona, dealt with the car, looked for an apartment and found one in a large, three-story house near Central Avenue that also served as a private retirement home. They liked my dad, frankly, and welcomed having someone to rent to who was self-sufficient. My studio apartment was the only one on the ground floor, and the only one with a kitchen, tiny though it was. I don't remember ever seeing anyone else there other than the owners . . . but I'm getting ahead of myself.

I had discussed this opportunity with Tom. We'd been together for about a year at that point. He knew I wanted to dance, and he was all for me spreading my wings.

With the single-mindedness of a typical teenager, I packed up my stuff but left my childhood dresser and twin bed behind, since the apartment came fully furnished and was so small there really wasn't room for them.

I gave no thought to leaving my brother without a roommate, without someone who could pay half the rent and utilities.

I lasted in Phoenix for just under two months. When the ballet company decided they didn't have the money to pay their dancers after about six weeks, I knew I couldn't survive there without a paycheck. I confronted the woman in the office, demanded a t-shirt in recompense since she couldn't write me my paycheck and there were boxes of t-shirts stacked behind her (hey, it was something), and promptly moved back home. Literally back home, to my parents' house, because when I called Dad to rescue me and pick up another rental trailer, Scott had acquired a roommate and I was told I would not be moving back in with him. Which was totally fair.

Scott's new roommate was one of two or maybe three roommates he had before Donald Michael Kraig moved in on February 29, 1980. Don was Scott's last roommate; he lived with Scott for six years. After Don moved out, Scott lived alone.

Now that I think about it, I realize I never met Don, either. I know about Don because he later wrote a book about Scott, entitled *The Magical Life of Scott Cunningham* (Llewellyn, 2012).

It's funny how we don't understand the repercussions of our actions and decisions until decades later, when it is far too late to change anything.

A Gem among Stones: The Legacy of *Cunningham's Encyclopedia of Crystal, Gem & Metal Magic*

By Nicholas Pearson

The 1980s saw a profusion of books on occult, New Age, and spiritual topics. One particular genre from this era has always held a special place in my heart: the magic and healing power of crystals. I was fascinated by all the different approaches to the topic—some books were dedicated solely to traditional folklore and magic, while others relied on personal experience and channeled information. Still more took a pseudoscientific perspective, hoping to rationalize crystal power through technical jargon and science-based metaphors. While some texts were imminently practical, others danced in the theoretical, leaving praxis to the imagination of the reader. That so many perspectives could be shared by different authors about a singular crystal or gem both perplexed and intrigued me. Each page I read and every book I devoured helped me dig a little deeper into the magic of the mineral realm.

When I started my own crystal journey, books on the subject were few and far between in mainstream bookstores. Consequently, one of the first titles I ever picked up was *Cunningham's Encyclopedia of Crystal, Gem & Metal Magic*, and I fondly added it to my budding library. Something about Scott's book made me feel right at home. His melodic and expressive prose drew me in, and the arguments in favor of crystal power are simple, pragmatic, demonstrative. From the beginning he reminds us that stone magic has always been part of human history, and that one simply needs to try it to know that it works. So try it I did, and my life was better for it.

Cunningham's work with crystals and gemstones heralded a new age of crystal literature. I've yet to find a proper crystal encyclopedia published before his. Though some earlier works are encyclopedic in scope, none are organized in the same user-friendly A-to-Z format of *Cunningham's Encyclopedia*. It's the convention we've come to know and love in crystal books ever since, as shown by Melody's *Love Is in the Earth*, D. J. Conway's *Crystal Enchantment*, Judy Hall's *The Crystal Bible* series, or even in my own *Crystal Basics*. Scott's book also introduces at-a-glance correspondences, reference tables, and other devices that are standard today. I wholeheartedly believe that without *Cunningham's Encyclopedia* to reinvent and standardize the format of crystal books we may never have had so many other titles to treasure on the subject.

In some ways, *Cunningham's Encyclopedia* serves as a bridge between communities that were, and are, often at odds with one another. One only has to tour the pages of the annotated bibliography—one of this book's hidden treasures—to find that rock and gem, fossil and ore appeal to academics, storytellers, occultists, healers, and New Age philosophers alike. This doesn't just reflect how deep Scott dug to extract pearls of crystal wisdom; it illustrates how incredibly human it is to love stones and how gloriously quotidian magic can be (without losing its mystique) if we permit ourselves to weave it into everyday life.

Although it seems like such a natural choice to examine both occult and New Age sources in search of common ground, this wasn't always the case, and in doing so Cunningham acknowledges that there is room at the table for everyone, that we can find similarity and shared interest in our love for rock and gem. I imagine that this may have been a natural, if not subconscious, act for Scott as a queer magician. Learning how to belong, to cultivate chosen family, and exercise community care was, and remains, part of everyday life in both the queer and magical scenes. *Cunningham's Encyclopedia* is special because it found a way through opposing narratives and reconciled them in ways that built bridges, rather than rejecting or isolating one community from another. Above all, this subtle alchemy helped me feel seen when I didn't feel as though I fit into any one place or another, and so I've endeavored to follow Scott's lead with my work today by welcoming all.

There is more to Cunningham's legacy beyond innovative literary conventions and clever, inclusive research. Scott displays a certain perspicacity that cuts through fluff and distills his own wisdom. He traces the common threads and deftly illustrates how uncomplicated—and effective—crystal magic and healing can be. The approach is solid, workable, reproducible; it's simple without being unsophisticated. Scott also doesn't restrict himself to medieval sources and gems known to the ancients. Rather, he embraces stones that were new and exciting in his day, ones that likely had little written lore before *Cunningham's Encyclopedia*. This introduced a spectrum of New Age crystals (like kunzite, sugilite, lepidolite, boji stones, and rhodonite) to the magical world, while simultaneously encouraging healers and metaphysicians to be better acquainted with the classics of stone magic, including fossils, holey stones, and salt.

As a twentieth-century folk magician, Scott is unparalleled, leaving no stone unturned in his exploration of mineral magic. There's a reason so many people, like myself, find *Cunningham's Encyclopedia of Crystal, Gem & Metal Magic* invaluable in our quest for crystal knowledge. Scott's words highlight his appreciation for the mineral realm and speak to his ability to see the magic all around us. He empowers us to try out crystal magic firsthand and encourages us to seek answers in the voices of the stones themselves. Magic and healing abound, from the humblest of pebbles to the finest gem, and we need only learn to seek it. My hope is that Scott's wisdom will guide the next generations to listen to these hidden voices and lift crystal magic to new heights.

LOS ANGELES, MARRIAGE, AND MAGICAL
HERBALISM—1980S

In the summer of 1979, I had already left California Ballet Company. It's amazing the blinders you must wear when you're in a rigorous physical field like ballet. Suddenly the restrictions were too much; when the Romanian ballet master got into my face about my yawning during a morning class, I'd had enough. I may have shouted some expletives back at him and quit, there and then. I was doing summer stock at Starlight Opera, and still living at home. Tom was dancing in a movie up in Los Angeles that summer—I think it was Steven Spielberg's *1941,* so we didn't get to see each other much, just snatched hours here and there when he had a weekend free.

During one of his free weekends, Tom asked me to marry him. My mother was ecstatic, considering I had already planned to move up to Los Angeles with Tom in a couple of months, as soon as the summer stock season was over.

She sat on my bed and took my hands after I told her. "Call me old-fashioned, but I'm so glad you've gotten engaged before you move up to L.A."

"Mom." I rolled my eyes.

She wiped happy tears from hers. "I get to plan your wedding!"

"We'll keep it simple. I promise."

"I don't care. When do you want to go wedding dress shopping?"

While I was happy with her response overall, I was so not ready for her all-in enthusiasm.

Life was good. Mom was happy, Dad was happy. Even Scott was happy for me, when I told him on the phone.

"Tom and I are getting married."

"Not surprised, but good for you. I've always liked him. He gets my jokes and innuendo, and fires right back at me."

"He's done a lot of musical theater. Of course, he gets your jokes and innuendo." Again, I rolled my eyes.

The day of our wedding was chosen as the first Saturday after my birthday, which ended up being February 23, 1980. Tom absolutely refused to marry a teenager and wanted to wait until I'd at least hit the age of twenty.

That morning, after the wedding rehearsal and breakfast, Scott took me aside before I got dressed.

He held my shoulders and really looked at me. "You sure you want to do this? I can drive the getaway car if you want to get away. You know, to somewhere that Calgon can't take you."

"Ha ha. Of course, I want to do this."

"Why?"

I thought for a moment. "Because when I looked into the future, I could see us in a home office somewhere, both of us with gray hair and wrinkles, banging away at our typewriters and taking care of each other. That's why."

He smiled and gave me a hug. "That's good enough for me."

◊◊◊

Scott, 1981.

In the summer of 1982, Scott came up to Los Angeles to speak at a few bookstores. He'd just published *Magical Herbalism.* Someone else picked him up from the airport and squired him around to his gigs. I picked him up from his last speaking gig, and he spent the night with me.

It was so good to see him. He was slightly astonished at the apartment. We were living in the San Fernando Valley, our third place there. It was small, but we got the place because Tom was going on tour with *The Pirates of Penzance,* the Gilbert and Sullivan comic opera, and I was going to be on my own, so it was fine. Security building, second floor, corner apartment. I made us dinner and he made jokes about my cooking (I've gotten a *lot* better at cooking since then, I swear). He was tired, though, so we didn't stay up too late. He took the really rather terrible couch and a blanket and didn't mind a bit.

The next day I took him to my favorite breakfast place before I drove him to the airport. Now, mind you, I hated driving to LAX, and I was still unhappy about driving the freeways. Scott knew that and he talked me into taking Sepulveda Boulevard all the way down to the airport. That's a really long drive, by the way, but we had a fantastic time. He kept saying things like . . .

"The freeway is right there, Legs. Oh look, there's an on-ramp."

"No."

"But you could."

Silence for a while.

"Oh look, another on-ramp."

Laughing. "No."

"There's another one."

By this time, it's a game, and I'm giggling and having a hard time catching my breath.

"Oh look, Chris. There's . . ."

"You're the one who looked it up in the Thomas Guide and said I should take Sepulveda all the way down. So that's what we're going to do." It took me a while to get those words out between giggles, but I finally did.

"I'm giving you options, Legs. Just giving you options."

◊◊◊

In 1982, Scott was diagnosed with Burkitt's lymphoma, a form of non-Hodgkin's lymphoma. He had a lump in his neck that grew quickly. He was treated at UC San Diego Medical Center. When the lump was finally removed, it was about the size of a baseball. He spent time recuperating at the parents' house, as well as at his apartment. I don't know details about his treatment. I don't know what happened, at all; I only know the diagnosis and that he recovered.

This scared me. But at the same time, it didn't feel real. Partly because I didn't do well with sick people and didn't visit him at all because at twenty-three, I was young and afraid for my brother and selfish, as many young people can be. And partly because he didn't like people seeing him when he was ill, and often told me not to visit. I don't believe we ever discussed his cancer. Whenever I talked to him on the phone and asked how he was doing, he would say he was all right. I chose to believe him, rather than poke at him.

He ended up conquering his cancer; he told me once, years later, that he used a lot of visualization and I bet he did some spell work, as well. We had no idea at the time that Scott was showing symptoms of AIDS. Hepatitis at seventeen. Lymphoma at twenty-seven.

There are some people who were close to him who might be angry with me for sharing his health issues. The fact is, Scott is gone, and has been for three decades. He doesn't care what people know about his health at this point.

If I knew secrets of the traditions he studied, those I would absolutely keep to myself. But I don't know those things. I don't know who he studied with, what his favorite rites and rituals were, beyond what he's shared in his books, or what other people have shared. I'm sharing the Scott I grew up with, laughed with, lost, and love with all my heart. Most of the time, anyway. Hey, siblings don't always get along. Even after one of them has passed away. Have you ever argued with someone who's dead? Yeah, it's a thing.

The next few years, Scott and I crossed paths at holidays at the parents' house, or whenever he had a speaking gig in Los Angeles, or when I came down to visit the folks. Dad would always proudly tell me whenever Scott had a new book out. We all were there for our parents' thirtieth wedding anniversary celebration in 1983.

In 1985, I hosted the family for Thanksgiving dinner. Scott and my parents drove up for the day. This was the first time I'd hosted the family for Thanksgiving, though not the first time I had cooked Thanksgiving dinner. Tom's brother David and his wife Cynthia were also there; they stayed at a nearby hotel, as they had planned to go to Disneyland later that weekend.

We lived in what used to be the Parish house, behind what used to be a church. Two women bought the property and turned the church

Greg, Christine, and Scott, thirtieth wedding
anniversary celebration, 1983.

into the Megaw Theater, a ninety-nine-seat Equity Waiver house, on the corner of Texhoma and Saticoy in Northridge. The Parish house was on Texhoma, while the church stood on Saticoy.

The church school buildings were turned into a costume shop/storage area and set storage. There was a beautiful, old (1896 or thereabouts) upright cherrywood piano with real ivory keys (chipped, but hey) in there with the set storage. At some point, they offered it to us just to get rid of it, and we snapped it up for about $400. We still have it. The piano gets a ritual cleaning/oiling twice a year or so.

The house was a proper house, with two bedrooms and a sort of den, plus a living room and a huge kitchen. When we first moved in during the summer of 1985, we painted and paneled and prettied up the place. We rescued a dog from the pound that we called Maggie, and we planted roses and felt very grown up about it all. I had just started a real job as a secretary at Candle Corporation, a privately held mainframe computer software company.

Scott was impressed. We lived in an actual house! With a yard, and a dog, and roses, and a guest room. He was happy to see us settled in, and even happier that I had a regular job with health benefits, something he never had.

It was a congenial time, that Thanksgiving gathering. No small kids yet. Just the people I loved, Maggie the puppy, and me, nervous about cooking for so many people. I had begun to really enjoy cooking, and I was determined the meal would be good. As I have no memories of anyone being sick afterward, I'll go with the assumption that all turned out beautifully.

Scott put up with the puppy, who wanted to sit in his lap. He was not a dog person, nor a cat person, for that matter, not knowing what to do with them, despite the fact that we grew up with dogs. He did thoroughly enjoy growing plants; we have farmer blood in us, after all.

As an aside—the Megaw Theater is no more. The ladies sold the land, and a developer ended up building condominiums on the site.

A Legacy of Kindness

By Lynne Redd

Life is funny—sometimes it's ha-ha funny, and other times you think Mother Nature is off her meds. Honestly, I am not sure which category this falls into, if either. Many years ago, before it was cool, I was introduced to the internet. It came at a time when I needed it the most. I am Southern—read that as repressed Southern and it will make more sense. I was not permitted to look into ideas that were against "God," or the "church." Keep in mind *this* church in the Southern Baptist Convention actually left the SBC when told they had to allow nonwhite people to be members. I started to look at other ideas, mostly Paganism. I looked into ideas of magic and shaping my own place where I was comfortable and accepted. Message boards on the internet led me to the same person over and over—Scott Cunningham.

A lot of people give me a funny look when I mention his name—even now, almost thirty years later. One of those people is Christine Ashworth. I did not have any idea that the sweet woman in California that I called sister was actually Scott's little sister, not until she posted that she was going through her books and mentioned his name. It brought up so many memories, including the voice in my head that is associated with Scott; *treat everyone you meet with dignity and respect.* It does not matter if this is in magical practice, or the person next to you on the plane. Everyone deserves dignity and respect.

For many years, I stayed quiet and just listened to the voices in my head that tell me which way to go—always one of three. Scott is one; the other two are my grandmother Temperance and my Nona from Sicily. All these people adopted me as family after seeing mine. Each had a lesson to teach: Nona on how to find the best in everyone even when they hurt you over and over; Grandmother Temperance that my heritage is in my blood no matter how far I repress it, hide it, or actively try to pretend I am something else. You cannot change who you are at the most basic level.

Scott's lesson was simply "be kind."

I was lucky at the time to have a small haven of people I have mainly lost track of over the years that were safe. Safe meant you could say anything, and they would smile, nod, get upset, or hand you the tissues. Sometimes it was all of the above. Scott was originally not a member of our online message board, until someone asked him a question and he joined to settle the argument. I honestly don't remember what the argument was about, but he stayed. The message board and the small group of people there were a haven long before safe havens became prevalent. No one was judging who you loved, how you loved, if you were political; just that you were kind.

The first signed copy I ever had of any book was *Magical Herbalism.* When I couldn't find it locally, Scott sent me a copy. I remember getting upset because I wasn't able to pay him for it. I had cash, but cash wasn't really safe in the mail. The book came to me with a note I have since passed on that said: *someone else will need help, make sure they get it.* All these years later, I wish I had kept the note; instead, I folded it up with a ten dollar bill and handed it to someone who had her credit card declined for a prescription. I am sure she did something similar. Every person I know has the same universal view of Scott—he was a lot ahead of his time. His personal politics or love interests aren't something I knew or even cared about. What mattered was how he could tell a simple story and the way the whole room would get quiet because everyone was listening. I would give everything I have and then some to just hear him laugh again. I really hope he knows that we appreciated how generous he was with his time. He wrote back—to all of us.

CHAPTER SEVEN

Our Thirties

1990S—BIRTH AND DEATH

In November 1990, Scott met my firstborn son, Chester. He didn't really know what to do with babies. Now that I think about it, he held my firstborn much the same way Grandma Hazel did . . . diffidently, absently, a smile for the photograph but then he quickly handed the baby back to me.

In 1991, Grandma Hazel Mae Cunningham died on Valentine's Day. She had just visited us in early December of 1990. I have photos of her with my baby son, in our condo on Saticoy Street in Van Nuys. I'd never hosted her before; she slept in the baby's room, on a foldup twin bed. I was nervous, and I remember I was making a fancy chicken pot pie from *Food & Wine* magazine.

"Dinner won't be done until eight, Grandma. Can I get you any-thing? Fruit, a cookie, water?"

Just then, the baby started to cry. I was hot, nervous, worried, and wanted to cry, too. Nothing about making that meal was going well. "I'm sorry. I'll just go change him. I'll be right back."

"Don't fuss, Chris." She was quite sharp. "I'm not going to wither and die if I don't eat supper at six. Don't fuss."

Somehow, that steadied me, and we ended up having a lovely dinner after all.

To this day, when I get in that weird, flustered mood, I can hear Grandma Hazel say, "Don't fuss, Chris."

Until I moved to Los Angeles in 1979, I was Chris to all and sundry, Chrissy to my parents. Los Angeles made it possible for me to be Christine. At this point, only a couple very special people still call me Chris.

I made the trip up for Grandma's memorial service, this time with my firstborn, baby Chet. We stayed in a hotel room, as Grandma's tiny rental house was full; my dad's sister Aunt Janie and Uncle Lyn were staying there. Having a baby with me during this sad time was fun. Uncle Lyn gave Chet his first French fry. That was also Chet's first solid food. To this day it makes me giggle.

My parents mailed a box to their house of my grandmother's dolls and stuffed animals that she'd made over the years. One of those, a brown bear about the size of a two-year-old, was what Scott picked out to live with him. My guess is he chose the bear because it fit with his aesthetic, as Grandma's clowns and dolls did not. He had given me his Gonk long ago, and though he had some Christmas ornaments from Grandma, and his Kitchen Witch, he didn't have much else from her.

The bear had soulful button eyes and was made from two different shades of brown faux fur. Grandma found the faux fur fiddly to work with, but she always said a bear wasn't a bear without fur. Scott kept the bear on his bed during the day.

Scott was in Hawai'i during this time. It wasn't until he got home that he learned his beloved Grandma Hazel had passed away.

Scott and I wrote letters and sent silly cards back and forth, because we had been raised that phone calls were expensive. So expensive, that in the 1960s and 1970s, my father only called his parents up in Oregon on Christmas and maybe their birthdays. Always, those calls happened after seven at night, preferably on a Sunday when the long-distance rates went down.

Even after phone rates went down in general, we still didn't call "just to talk." Someone had to be sick or dead, or some good news needed to be shared. We did not call "just to check in." Even after cell phones became a thing, we did not call just to check in. Even now, my brother Greg and I do not call each other on a regular basis.

We were trained, from an early age, to not call. Calling someone now is nothing. Back then, a five-minute long-distance call during regular rates could cost ten dollars. That's a lot of money when you have three kids and are supporting your entire family with your freelance writing. The only time Dad made long-distance calls during daylight were when he needed to talk to his editors in New York City, and even then, he would call around six in the morning, off peak hours.

Scott, Mom, Grandma Hazel, and Grandpa Merle, 1977.

I mention it because I received a lot of pushback from my parents' last caregiver for not calling them on a daily basis. Often, your training outweighs your understanding of reality. I also got pushback for not being there when Dad had shoulder surgery. I had a full-time job. He had a caregiver. He basically told me not to come, which I'm grateful for since I would have had to take vacation time for it and wouldn't have had much to do while there.

I told Dad, years later, not to come when I had brain surgery. Because what could he do, other than be uncomfortable in our house that didn't have a guest room, and worry?

If I had been a more prominent presence in their household, would I have been able to change the course of our lives? If I had called more frequently, driven down to see them more often, then perhaps I would have been able to be there when Mom passed away. It would have been me, perhaps, holding her hand and telling her I loved her as her eyes closed a final time.

Instead, I am left with the memory of visiting them two weeks before her death. MS and a series of TIAs had robbed my mother of her mobility the year after Scott died, and by 2007, most of her speech was garbled. We had little to say to one another, as usual those last few years. I couldn't understand many of the words that came out of her mouth, and she had severe hearing loss but no hearing aids, as her fingers couldn't have dealt with the complexity.

My mother had "her" chair. Over the years it had changed, but it was always a chair she could read in and be comfortable in, right there near the hallway, but where she could easily watch TV as well.

When her walking became unsteady, they bought a lift chair that also reclined. It was this chair that she sat in on our last Sunday together. I huddled into her. She sat swaddled in a blanket as she was almost always cold. She looked so small, so lost, until I caught her gaze and we both smiled. Everything was fine, until it wasn't. I put my head in her lap and I cried. I felt she was already straddling that line between this world and the next.

Her fingers gently combed through my hair. She patted my back, and when I finally lifted my head, I saw tears on her cheeks as well. I kissed her. Told her I loved her. Hugged her close, one more time, before I had to drive the three plus hours to home.

Perhaps if I had spent more hours on the road between our houses, called more often, been more of a presence in their lives, maybe I wouldn't have gotten a call on a Saturday, telling me Mom had been in the hospital for the past six days with a UTI that would not go away. Her nerve endings had long since burned out, and she did not feel any pain; but the infection got away from them. I was in a comedy writing class at Second City when the call came, around two thirty PM. Dad told me not to come; then her caregiver called four hours later, when I was at work at Coldwater Creek. She had died of sepsis.

If I had gone, I could have held her hand. I could have kissed her once more. Instead, I listened to what Dad said and didn't go to see her. I feel guilty for listening. For doing as Dad had wished rather than what my heart told me. But for whatever reason, I was not supposed to be there at her side.

It's taken me a long time to come to that understanding.

I share this about Mom because Scott loved her so. They had a solid bond between them. While he lived, he took care of her, was always so thoughtful, bringing her flowers, running errands, and paying her due attention. I have no doubts whatsoever that Scott, fourteen years after he passed away and during this time period when Mom was so sick, visited her frequently in spirit in the days before her death.

HOLIDAYS

Mom loved celebrating the holidays. From heart-shaped cakes and cookies at Valentine's Day, to strawberry shortcake for breakfast on

April Fool's Day, baskets and stories for Easter, July Fourth hamburgers and her special red-white-and-blueberry dessert, Halloween treats, a Thanksgiving that groaned with turkey and all the typical sides, plus the Christmas cookies, fudge, and rocky road candy, holidays almost always meant yummy, seasonal food, and household decorations, and Scott especially looked forward to those treats that marked the seasons.

Now that I think about it, marking the season changes has always been a family tradition. It started for us in September, when it was back-to-school time. New clothes, haircuts, pads of paper, new pencils and pens, all things that our office-supply-loving family enjoyed.

Out of all the holidays, though, Halloween was Scott's favorite, even as a little kid. He loved carving pumpkins into scary jack o' lanterns, and picking a pumpkin was a serious endeavor. I have vague memories of him in a TV set costume —a box he wore with a painted "screen" and knobs on it, with an antennae hat; unfortunately, my dad wasn't big on photos of us at Halloween, so there are none.

Samhain/Halloween was probably Scott's very favorite holiday as he got older. When we were younger, it was all about the costume and the candy, and for a while, the fun Halloween fair at the grade school. When he got older, it was all about the decorations, and his own private preparations. Before we moved out of the house, he would frequently be gone all Halloween day and night, not returning until the wee hours of the morning.

Thanksgivings were when Dad would get us all together and set up his Rolleiflex camera on the tripod, set the timer, and take our family photo for the annual Christmas cards and letters they'd send out. Every year, he'd have them printed up and then he'd frame the best one and put it up on the wall in the entrance hallway. Dad was always the photographer at any gathering.

Scott would help chop the onions and celery for the stuffing, and the night before, he and I would flip a coin to see who got to make the

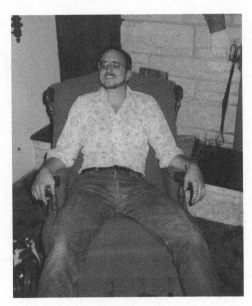

Scott resting easy.

cranberry sauce from scratch. We used to put a spoonful of the hot sauce over a scoop of vanilla ice cream, for a once-a-year treat.

That last Thanksgiving, we were at Greg's place for dinner. Baby Chet took to Scott and would stand and babble at his knee. Scott talked back to him.

Christmas Day, we kids were up at five AM like clockwork. Whichever kid woke up first woke up the rest, and then we all woke up the parents (well, when we were really little).

Before Dad had a fireplace built into the house, our stockings were hung on the lamps next to the couch and chairs. One year, Greg's stocking was against the light bulb and caught fire, leaving a hole in the toe of his stocking, which ended that practice. This was before I turned six and so is a faint and misty memory which I might have forgotten, but Greg's stocking forever carried that hole. He soon received a new stocking from the store.

Christmas, 1963. From left to right —Christine, Dad Chet, Scott,
Greg, Mom Rosie, and pupdog Skippy.

Our first stockings, by the way, were all handmade by Grandma
Hazel. My parents were grateful for them, for they were slender things
and not as huge as the ones you can currently find in stores.

Mom would always start her decorating on the mantel. She'd put
out white cotton batting for "snow" as the foundation. Then after carefully unwrapping the creche, she'd add that to the mantel. Decorations
Grandma Hazel had made also went up, and candles in the shape of
carolers. Greenery, and a wreath on the wall. The final touch was our
stockings.

We knew, once Mom decorated the mantel, purchasing and decorating the tree wouldn't be far behind. The best part of that was lying
under the tree after it was all lit up and decorated, and just gazing up at
the lights. Scott and I loved to do that.

Our Christmas trees always held a special magick. It had ornaments
that we kids made, ornaments that my parents had from the beginning
of their marriage, ornaments that Grandma Hazel made. A few were
bought every now and then, as breakage occurred. We also had icicles

back when they were made of lead, which we re-used as much as possible every year.

My parents would only put presents that came from relatives under the tree before Christmas. We kids would put our presents under the tree to each other and to the parents, so when we went to bed on Christmas Eve, there weren't many gifts there.

But the next morning was magick. Presents piled high and around. We knew it wasn't just Santa, who brought us small things. I have kept this tradition up, adding presents to the tree after the kids have gone to bed.

On Christmas morning, until the parents were awake, we were allowed to turn the tree lights on and dig into the delights of our Christmas stockings, but we were not allowed to touch the presents.

As soon as we made enough noise to wake her up, Mom would get up and make coffee, while we waited for Daddy to come out, as he was always last. He would wrap himself in his plaid wool dressing gown and come out at last to the living room. He'd sit by the fireplace, start a small fire, and wait while Scott and I took turns handing out presents.

We weren't a one-at-a-time family. Rather, we were a pile presents at everyone's feet and then open. Then pile, and open. On and on, until all the presents were gone. And as we always saved Grandma and Grandpa Cunningham's box for Christmas Day, even though we opened the package beforehand, there were always wrapped presents to open, in paper we didn't recognize.

Grandma's box was a delight. Often there would be a bag of hazelnuts tucked in, and sometimes homemade caramels. If Grandma included ornaments, she'd label that package "for the tree," and we'd open that one the day their box arrived.

She stopped sending a box once all us kids left home, and instead sent cards. Totally practical and in keeping with what I knew of her, but I missed the whimsy of her ornaments. Since my parents have passed on, I have acquired more of them, and they always decorate our tree.

Christine and Scott, Christmas 1982.

When we were growing up, my parents never had a lot of extra money. At the same time, they made sure we never felt any lack. (Dad had a line of credit on his checking account, so he wouldn't bounce checks. Important, when your income did not come in a regular pattern.) The Sears Christmas catalog was our dreaming ground, and we each used to circle and initial the things we'd like. Did we get them all? Hardly. But every now and then, yes, we'd get a couple of them.

It must have been around 1972 that Scott really got into wrapping presents at Christmas. He gave the most beautiful and artistically wrapped gifts. In 1973, he was also the one who decided to surprise our parents with their own Christmas stockings, buying them and filling them and not putting them up until very early Christmas morning. After that first year, I helped Scott fill the stockings. I carried that tradition into my marriage, sharing with my husband about Christmas stockings and what kind of presents to put into them—and now our sons contribute to our stockings.

Earlier Christmases . . . I remember Scott showing me, when I was about six or seven, just where mom used to hide the Christmas presents.

One year, I even looked at the unwrapped presents, and then felt so guilty that I never did that again. Luckily, I forgot what I had seen, until I saw them again when I unwrapped them. But man, older brothers!

Scott absolutely loved Christmas when we were young, and then that love found its way to Yule.

As he says in the preface to his book, *Earth Power* (Llewellyn, 1983):

From the earliest years of my life I have been attracted to Nature in all its manifestations. The sight of a field of blooming wildflowers, the texture of a granite cliff, the untamable fury of a prairie thunderstorm—these are some of my most vivid childhood impressions.

And . . .

Magic is the art of working with the forces of Nature to bring about necessary changes. That is magic, pure and simple.

Christmas, 1975.

Scott loved Nature. He loved the changing of the seasons, and he loved Yule, the longest night of the year. Through his years of searching out knowledge of the natural world, he found magick and he found that the tools of such knowledge lie all around us; we have only to pay attention.

I do not know when Scott turned from the church teachings and toward Nature, but it seemed to be an easy progression that started when he was young and didn't ever become a big deal in the family. Until he was nineteen, he sang in the church choir with our mom, and I believe he did so because it made her happy. By then he was a few years into learning and growing in the ways of magick.

The first year after Scott had left Orange Avenue, maybe 1989, he had an apartment just a couple miles from the parents. It was fairly roomy and a lot nicer than the one on Orange Avenue. He even had a balcony where he grew an amazing number of plants in a small space.

He invited Tom and me over one evening after dinner when we were in town, just the three of us, to celebrate Yule, though it was before the actual day. Scott had a live tree, and the lights . . . oh, the lights on the tree were totally crazytown, and totally Scott.

The lights had a switch that could alter the rate of flashing, and the three of us sat and talked and laughed and had a great time without the parents, without anyone else there, in his home lit by the lights of his Yule tree.

I can still see the lights from the tree twinkling in the large lenses of his glasses, lighting up his face as he discussed astronomy with Tom, talking about telescopes and travelers of all sorts navigating by the stars at night.

Later, after he died, I was given those lights, and for the longest time we used them on our tree every year until they finally wore out. I still can't believe he's been gone for so long now.

In *Cunningham's Book of Shadows* (Llewellyn, 2009), Scott discusses the sabbats of Wicca, and he starts with Yule. I know that many Wic-

cans and witches believe the New Year begins on the day after Halloween, which is also called Samhain by witches, Wiccans, and Pagans;
but to me, that's still the winding down of the year. Yule, with the
celebration of returning light, is more in keeping with new beginnings.
It was a comfort to me to read that he had the same thought, though
not expressed in quite the way I expressed it here.

I wish he hadn't been quite so discreet, so circumspect with his
witchery. But I also understand why he did what he did. In the '70s, it
was barely acceptable for men to have long hair. To be gay *and* interested in witchcraft and Wicca? Not acceptable. So he hid in plain sight,
as so many have done before him. It still makes my heart ache. How I
wish he could be here, now, and see how far we have come . . . and yet,
I'm sure his heart would break at how far we have still to go.

CHAPTER EIGHT

Food, Home, and Pine Trees

1992–1993—HOME AGAIN

When Scott moved back to our parents' home in the autumn of 1992, he brought his iron bedstead that he loved, in spite of the fact that the supports for the mattress were soldered upside-down so there was no way to keep the mattress solidly on the frame. He had a hag stone that he'd found at Hagstone Cove attached to the headboard with a rope he'd hand-crocheted out of blue yarn. (A hag stone is a stone that has had a hole worn clear through it by the sea. In the last decade or so, I have been fortunate to find a few hag stones of my own.) He brought some incense and a few packed boxes, half a closet of clothes, and very few other things.

Scott had given up his apartment, had a private "sale" of his things to friends and loved ones for minor amounts of money, and sold or gave many things away as well. Books, crystals, shells, he had shed most of his belongings in preparation of what was to come.

Many of his books, author copies given to him by his publishers, he'd brought to Dad's house over the years, lacking the space for them. Out in the family room (our converted garage), Dad had made a huge bookshelf dedicated to all the copies of Scott's books, as well as those that no one bought during his sale or that he hadn't given away. Dad stapled heavy-duty plastic across the top of the bookcase and draped it to the floor, to keep those books as dust-free as possible. With Dad's blessing, I snagged many books over the years and gave many away to friends.

◊◊◊

In February 1993, Scott was moved from home to the hospital, and then after it was decided more chemicals would not help him get better, he was moved to a nursing home. My dad urged us to come visit, as he wasn't sure how much time Scott had. We drove the three hours with our son Little Chet, left him with my parents, and went to see Scott.

There are good nursing homes, and not-so-good nursing homes. In my opinion, he was in a not-so-good nursing home. The noise of people in pain, the smells, the fog of anger and despair from patients and visitors alike hit me physically when we walked into the place. We were directed to his room, one that could have held three people, but he was alone. A nurse straightened his bedsheets and talked to him about lunch. By this time, he was totally blind. Totally bedridden.

The nurse started to go, but he asked for his bear, his voice slightly frantic. The bear made by Grandma Hazel, that he'd picked out from those that Mom and Dad had brought home after Hazel's death just two years earlier. The nurse had set it on the chair while she worked, and now she handed it to him. A good two feet tall and about sixteen inches wide, that bear was Scott's touchstone, had sat on his bed at home and at Dad's house, and had been the one thing he'd taken with him to the hospital and then to hospice. He clutched it to his chest.

It was finally time for us to make ourselves known.

He turned his face to me when I spoke his name. His eyes were unseeing, and he didn't wear glasses. His face, darkened and sunken with disease, looked like a stranger's. His body, once so healthy, reminded me of the photos I had seen that showed victims in a concentration camp. His voice, however, was the same, if slightly weakened.

I had brought sandalwood lotion, thinking at least the smell would be comforting. I asked if he would like me to rub it into his hands and arms, and he said please. The three of us made small talk about how long he'd have to be there.

"I don't want to stay here."

"I don't blame you. Home is better." I smoothed the lotion into the dry skin of his hands and forearms, his finger and wrist bones prominent, massaging the muscles.

I sighed. "I'm sorry I wasn't there at Christmas. I feel like I let you down."

"Don't be stupid."

I smiled and sighed again. "Do you want lotion on your feet, too?"

"Yes, please. It feels good."

I massaged it gently into his feet and ankles, but all too soon I was done.

"I'm tired. I think I'll nap." His sightless gaze darted around the room and he moved restlessly, clutching the bear to his chest.

I held his hand. "I'm leaving the lotion here for you, on the table. I love you." I kissed him on the forehead.

"I love you too, Legs."

I left without looking back.

We hadn't been there more than twenty minutes, total. I had managed to not break down in his presence. But the minute we left that place, out on the sidewalk, I lost it, and cried in my husband's arms. I am crying as I write this. I am sure that when I re-read this, I will cry. Those memories are etched into my heart. And while they hurt, I am so glad I have them.

On the trip back to my parents' house, I cursed that nursing home viciously. In my mind, it was a horrible place. With the passage of time,

I so want to believe that the staff were caring and doing the best they could; but in the end, nothing makes up for the fact that he was there to begin with.

While Scott was in the nursing home, Dad found a lawyer who would draw up Scott's last will and testament, pro bono. This same lawyer later drew up Mom and Dad's family trust and was there to help us close it after Dad passed away in 2017. Scott made Dad the executor of his estate, and five of us were his beneficiaries and hold all the rights to his published works. Greg and I are two of those five. For privacy reasons, the other three will go unnamed. For the record, I do not have a copy of Scott's will. I have never read Scott's will. I do not know what was in Scott's will, other than who, along with Greg and me, were designated as beneficiaries.

A few days after our visit to the nursing home, Dad called me to say they were bringing Scott home for hospice care. He would be on fewer medications, most of them for pain. Dad said he'd take lessons on how to care for him, how to administer the injections and whatnot, and they'd have a home health hospice nurse come by three times a week.

Scott wanted home. Both my parents wanted him home. Dad was sixty-five. Scott was thirty-six.

By this time, it was confirmed that I was pregnant with my second child, so that was a bright spot in 1993. Instead of morning sickness, however, I had random sickness. I'd never know when it would hit, which made that first trimester a difficult one.

We made one more visit while he was home. We didn't stay long. Scott wasn't what you'd call chatty, and my parents' grief was overwhelming. Having to watch him die was draining on Dad, and Mom looked constantly on the verge of tears even while she held out hope that he would recover.

I remember one time when Dad and I were in the kitchen, and he was exhausted. He said that Scott had gotten angry at the way Dad made scrambled eggs. Dad couldn't get them fluffy enough. Mom hadn't cooked for a few years, and Dad was still learning how. It was a difficult time on all three of them, and heartbreaking for my parents.

I understand now that Scott's anger was born of frustration at his own limitations. After all, it's kind of hard to cook when you can't see and can't stand up for very long, and he did enjoy cooking.

Dad was angry at "the gays" for getting Scott sick. It took him quite a few years to shed that thought pattern. We had many conversations where I said things like, *Daddy, do you really think someone chooses to be so different, when it is so hard to just survive the hatred thrown at them all the time?* We talked about the science behind it, as well. He finally did come to understand that human sexuality is not a choice. He made his peace with it.

MOM'S KITCHEN

As I mentioned, Scott and Mom had a close relationship. They would go to the movies together, usually movies no one else wanted to see. They were both excited to see *Theater of Blood* with Vincent Price and Diana Rigg. I remember this mainly because I kept hearing "The Udder of Blood" instead of "Theater of Blood," and I just didn't get it until I saw the ticket stub, with the name of the movie spelled out.

Horror movies, campy monster movies, musicals, those were what Mom and Scott enjoyed. In his late teens, he started hanging out in the kitchen with her, helping her cook dinner, making cookies and cakes, learning the whole how-to-feed-himself thing.

Later, of course, when he was writing his book *The Magic in Food*, he returned to Mom's kitchen.

She wasn't the best of cooks, but she wasn't all potato chips on top of casseroles made with canned cream of whatever soup, either. She'd have been horrified, honestly, about putting potato chips on top of casseroles, though she did use crushed cornflakes for baked fried chicken, which I have to admit was tasty. Alas, neither my mother, in her time, nor I so far have managed to master true fried chicken.

Mom loved Chinese food, but she never tried to make it. She collected recipes from Grandma Hazel and Dad's sister Janie, shared recipes with church and P.E.O. friends, culled recipes through magazines and the local paper, and owned a whole bunch of cookbooks, many of which later made it to my own kitchen. Scott would go with her to our local Chinese restaurant; those were special dates they had together.

Mom made a wicked-good Triple Lemon Cake that we all loved and went to almost every Methodist potluck. From Thanksgiving to just before Christmas, she would spend days making Christmas cookies and candy treats. Food was one way she showed her love, and even now I miss her cookies. I feel bad that I rarely bake cookies, as both Mom and my Grandma Hazel were champs at it. But I will say, I share love every time I cook for my family and friends, and I cook dinner every night for my family, so we have that in common.

We'd have an overcooked triangular pot roast almost every Sunday. To this day, I can't stand that cut of meat, but it was cheap. Probably still is. She'd also make beef gravy from scratch, which made it taste much better, and always mashed potatoes, my favorite. Beef for five was expensive, so we usually only had it once a week—twice, if there was a good sale. She'd make hamburger casserole (but no potato chips on top!), lasagna as a treat, Swiss steak, or pork chops if they were on sale; meatloaf or the aforementioned baked "fried" chicken were staples, as well as that triangular pot roast. Chef Boyardee pizza in a box was a special treat—one box of cheese pizza, one box of pepperoni—as we almost never went out to eat at a restaurant, and we never had pizza delivered. I believe my first non-Chef Boyardee pizza was in New York City, during the Epic Vacation.

Scott learned how to make my mother's macaroni and cheese (more cheese. No, *more* cheese!) from scratch. No blue box at our house. We were adults before we realized people could make mac 'n cheese from a box bought at the grocery store. He also learned how to make the lasagna recipe she loved, which was in one of the San Carlos United Methodist Church's book of recipes. It's the one recipe from back in the day that I still make, only now I use ricotta instead of cottage cheese. I can make that dish by instinct at this point.

Mom had a Midwest style of cooking. She shied away from spices, other than salt, pepper, basil, oregano, and parsley. (Baking was a different story.) She never made shrimp or steak, mostly because they couldn't afford it. A salad at every meal was a must. Garlic was not a thing in her world, though she might have had garlic salt in the cupboard.

Dad did most of the cooking whenever there was fish, usually because he caught it. Dad loved to go deep sea fishing, and a half-day boat trip usually ended with him bringing home halibut, bass, or every now and then, yellowfin tuna—but that was the exception. Scott went fishing with Dad once or maybe twice, but it wasn't his thing; up before dawn, and the hours on the boat were long and not always exciting. Scott did love being on the water, though, and counted his time near the ocean as precious.

Our parents weren't fans of spicy foods, and meals tended to be "all-American" in the 1950s' way in flavor. I am certain that Scott's palate expanded once he was away from home, as mine did; but when we were kids, we just weren't exposed to spicy foods.

Dad did all of the outside grilling, and a lot of the outdoor cooking when we camped. He taught all of us how to light coals, and how to use the outdoor grill. Whenever it came to fire, Dad was the master. Campfire, or coals, he was there, handling it all. We kids learned from a young age how to lay a fire so it would catch and burn well. To this day, when I scent campfire smoke, or if my clothes smell of campfire smoke, I get nostalgic for my family.

Scott and I didn't cook meals for the family. Scott did bake, though. Brownies and cookies and cakes. I remember one time he was experimenting with different types of bread. Not all of those recipes turned out the way he'd hoped, but we'd always enjoy whatever he offered.

Any time one of us got the hankering for sweets, out would come the mixing bowl. Scott's favorite cookies to make were Mom's *Gigantor* cookies, a recipe she got from Grandma Hazel back in the early 1960s. These cookies brought back memories of Saturday morning cartoons and yummy scents from the kitchen. Store-bought cookies were rare in our house.

THE TALL TREES

In early August 2007, Greg and I and our families went camping up at Mammoth, at Sherwin Creek. Greg's son Matthew and his wife Sara and their two kids, who also live in the San Diego area, picked up Dad and brought him with them.

Rosie had passed away in April of that year. Chet, seventy-nine at the time, was having a difficult time walking on a bum ankle, a gift from his running and racquetball days, but he loved being in the mountains, loved having his family around him. I remember he got out of the car and breathed deep, looked up at the towering pines.

"Daddy! I'm glad you guys made it." I gave him a hug.

He slung his arm around my shoulder and looked around. "It's good to be back among the tall trees. It's been . . ."

He didn't continue; he didn't have to. The last time we were among tall trees, barely a month earlier, we had scattered Mom's ashes up on the ridgeline behind the Cabin, in the same spot where we'd scattered Scott's ashes.

I slid my arm around him and leaned my head on his shoulder. "I'm so glad you're here."

"I'm glad to be here, Chrissy."

Mom's Gigantor Cookies (named for the 1960s' cartoon)

Ingredients:

1 cup brown sugar

1 cup white sugar

1 cup shortening

2 eggs

1 tsp maple extract

2 cups flour

2 tsp baking soda

1 tsp baking powder

½ tsp salt

2 cups cornflakes

2 cups oats

1 cup chopped pecans

OPTIONAL:

½ to 1 cup unsweetened shredded coconut

1 cup chocolate chips

Preheat the oven to 350° Fahrenheit. Cream shortening and sugars until mixed well. Add eggs and beat until smooth. Add in maple extract.

In a separate bowl, combine flour, baking soda, baking powder, and salt. Blend together and add this mixture to the wet ingredients. Stir with a wooden spoon until well combined. Add in cornflakes, oats, and nuts. Stir well. (This is also where you'd add the chocolate chips and/or coconut if you want.)

Drop by tablespoon onto a cookie sheet that has been greased or sprayed with cooking oil. Bake for ten to fifteen minutes, depending on your oven. This recipe makes between ten to two dozen cookies, depending on how big you make each cookie.

The fire ring—well, let's just say, there were four Cunninghams there (Dad, Greg, me, and Matthew, Greg's son), plus my two boys who, when it comes to fire, are also Cunninghams in that we like playing with it, adding to it, poking it, and get very territorial.

My husband looked at us around the fire and just stepped back and laughed as we argued about whose turn it was to poke/add wood/play with it.

His advice? "Never come between a Cunningham and their fire." Wise words, indeed.

At night, after dinner was over and the dishes were done, we sat and watched the flames. We didn't talk about Rosie, or about Scott, but I could feel them there with us. With Mom so recently gone, I didn't look to see what story the flames held for me that vacation. I didn't want to know.

Dad didn't talk much about Scott after he died. Every now and then, when communications from Scott's publisher arrived, Dad would call and we'd chat. One of the conversations I remember vividly is below.

"Hey Chrissy."

"Hi Daddy."

"You see that royalty statement yet?"

"I did. Very cool."

"If Scott were alive, I bet he'd have a house in Hawai'i."

That's how Dad always saw Scott, as living happily on one of the Hawai'ian Islands. I like to think a part of Scott is there now, enjoying life.

CHAPTER NINE

And He's Gone

MARCH 28, 1993

Oh help . . . it's the end of March, 2019. I've had a personal meltdown in my fiction writing life, so I'm turning back to this project. Started looking for photos (I have six boxes of photo albums), and they have caught me. Shaken me until I can barely see. Photos of Scott, so young, so happy, so silly. And then those awful photos . . . ironically, wearing the same short-sleeved, blue-striped shirt he wore in a photo from 1991, when he was healthy.

There's the photo of us, me hugely pregnant, in 1990. I'm wearing a pair of yellow overall shorts, a maternity outfit, and he's got his arm around me. We're both looking tired, but healthy.

Then there's the one of us at the cabin in 1968, I guess. I've got my Coca-Cola pants on, he's got long bangs, Mom's in front with the wooden sign Dad had made for the cabin. Pine Haven, the sign said. Greg was standing behind Mom, looking off in the distance. In a weird way, that photo could have been an album cover for a rock band, if you know what I mean.

There's the first Christmas photo after Greg got married, so it was just me, Scott, and the parents. Then there's my favorite photo of all time, the one of Scott and Dad, taken in Dad's den by a *Los Angeles Times* newspaper photographer for an article.

◊◊◊

The mind has many compartments, and our memories are kept in them. At any moment, when you go down a mental path, a memory box may spring out at you, willy-nilly and in no special order.

Today's memory box holds heartache. Sunday, March 28, 1993, I received a phone call, just a little before three PM. Dad was on the line, and he sounded tired and sad. Just hearing his voice, I knew.

Scott was not in any pain when he passed away. Dad told me how he would frequently get up in the middle of the night to check on Scott, who was bed-bound at that point.

Scott's books. The photographs. My
memories. Bits and pieces of a beautiful
soul, a beautiful life, interrupted by death.

Around three in the morning, on March 28, 1993, Scott called out when he heard Dad, and asked for a glass of water.

After taking the water from Dad, he drank, then set the glass down on the table beside his bed. The last words Dad heard him speak were simple. "Thank you, Dad."

When Dad got up the next morning, he checked on Scott before helping Mom get up. Scott had fallen into a coma and was unresponsive. Once Chet got Rosie up and dressed, she sat next to Scott's bed in her wheelchair, holding his hand, and they waited. Scott died at about two thirty PM that same day. Dad called me few minutes later.

"Hey Chrissy."

"Hi Daddy."

"Just want you to know that Scott died about twenty minutes ago. Rosie was holding his hand."

"Oh Daddy." Tears filled my eyes.

"I don't know what to do, who to call. The Oscars are on tonight, and we have neighbors coming over. I suppose I could just, uh, close the door and not tell anyone."

I didn't know whether to laugh or be horrified. "Daddy. Call the coroner's office or call nine-one-one. They'll be able to tell you what to do next."

"But it's Sunday. Are they open on Sundays?"

"The coroner's office probably doesn't have normal working hours, Daddy. Give them a call."

"Do you want to come down? I mean, I know it would be inconvenient since you have work tomorrow, but the Oscars are on and . . . you know."

I swiped at the tears on my cheeks. "I'm really not feeling too good. It's that morning sickness that's not just in the morning. I'm sorry."

Silence sat between us for a little bit.

"I'm sorry, Daddy. I'm so sorry he's gone. How's Mom?"

"Glad she was there to hold his hand. Crying. She misses you."

"I miss you guys, too. Let's hang up, and you call nine-one-one, okay?"

"Okay Chrissy. I love you."

"Love you too, Daddy. Hug Mom for me. Call me if you need me. I'll see you next weekend."

Even now, the memory of his uncertainty makes me smile through my tears. There was such an emptiness to his voice. He'd been both Mom and Scott's daily caregiver and now there was little else to do but focus on the next thing, and the next thing. And of course, tend to Mom.

This was back in the day of pagers. So, once I hung up, I paged my husband, who was performing as Peter Quince in *A Midsummer Night's Dream* at the Globe Playhouse in West Hollywood. When the pager went off, he told me later he had to make an entrance, so he thrust the pager at a close friend of ours and asked him to call me. Five minutes later, when our friend caught Tom's eye from across the stage, he merely shook his head. Tom knew, then, that Scott had passed on.

In 1990, when Scott was diagnosed with AIDS, I was three months' pregnant with my first child. In 1993, when Scott died, I was three months' pregnant with my second child. It has always struck me as significant. Hope during times of despair.

AFTERMATH

Dad decided that Scott would not want any sort of memorial service at the church (I disagreed). I don't know if he talked with Scott about it; but remembering my cousin Lori, who had died of a gunshot wound at the age of twenty, and my Uncle Kenny's rage and heartache at her death and the subsequent lack of memorial service for her, I figured Dad was following in his big brother's footsteps. There was no formal service or informal gathering put on by the family for the family and friends. No memorial. No nothing, and it gutted me.

I know that Scott believed that death is just another transition, just as birth is. Birth, death, rebirth—the cycle is continuous. I have come to believe this as well, but at the time I would have liked to participate in a more public mourning of the man, my brother, whom I loved.

The Pagan community in San Diego had not one, but two gatherings to honor Scott. I know our parents attended one, I believe the one at deTraci Regula's house, three days after Scott's death; but since our parents didn't let me or my older brother Greg know about it, we couldn't be there. I am still enraged and sad at the parents for making that decision for Greg and me; not that it truly matters at this point.

Scott's death, and the lack of a formal grieving ritual, affected me in ways that I'm still processing. There is a reason that grief rituals exist. There is a reason for memorial services, for gatherings, for wakes when someone dies. The living often need such rituals to process the loss of the loved one. It's really that simple. It doesn't have to be a church service. It doesn't have to be filled with people.

On our way down to see my parents the weekend after Scott had died, we stopped at a florist and bought three helium balloons—red, blue, and yellow—and when we got to Avenida de Pico in San Clemente, Tom took the off-ramp and got us to the beach. Along with our two-year-old, we released them at the beach, and said our formal goodbyes. My toddler was so excited to see all the sand, but he willingly held a balloon for a moment. Looking out at the surging and retreating Mother Ocean, I said a quiet prayer and we all let our balloons go, sending wishes and love to Scott, a dear soul.

It helped, and yet . . . Yes, I know, bad for the environment. We weren't exactly thinking about the environment at the time, and while I'm sure Scott would have scolded us for it, it felt right.

After the release of the balloons, I had the joy of watching my baby boy try to claim all the sand on the beach, the way he claimed all the sand in his turtle sandbox back home. Seeing him finally come to realize that there was *so much sand*, and that there was plenty for everyone, was such a joy.

Two months after Scott died, I went to a massage therapist that specialized in pregnancy massage. I was only five months' pregnant, yet I was quite uncomfortable. She asked me if there was anything I was upset about, and I mentioned Scott's recent death, and started crying. In her "wisdom," she told me that my grief would affect my child, and I needed to get rid of the grief or my child would be born deformed.

Horrified, I left her table without my massage, didn't go to work that day, and headed to the beach where I sat, crying and watching the waves. I remember talking to Scott. Praying that he was happy where he was, that he saw everything as it truly was, and that he knew how much I loved him. I'm pretty sure he knew that last part. (Oh, and my baby was born perfect. Two middle fingers way up to that massage therapist.)

I railed at God for taking Scott from us so fast. I cursed the AIDS virus, and how it had caught the medical community flat-footed in how to treat it. How politicians looked the other way, when they could have been much more proactive. Gosh, that sounds a lot like the very beginning of the COVID-19 pandemic, doesn't it?

I cursed the fact that the medical cocktails came too late to save his life.

Did I ever feel Scott's presence, after his death? Yes. The first time was in July 1993. We were in San Diego to scatter Scott's ashes. That was scheduled for Sunday, and on Saturday, since I was seven months' pregnant with baby number two, I went to nap on Scott's bed in my old room.

I was out. Down for the count. Slumbering deeply. Then I woke, and the bed was shaking. The hag stone Scott had attached to the headboard was clanging against the iron. I hung on, scared that it was an earthquake. Then I realized nothing else in the room was moving.

Kind of freaked out, once the bed stopped shaking, I got up and went to join my parents, husband, and our son Chet. When I asked if we'd had an earthquake, the response, of course, was no. I knew then that Scott had been saying, "Hey there, everything's fine, Legs."

It brought me a huge measure of peace. In retrospect, maybe he was saying, "Wake *up*, woman! You have work to do!" But at the time I did not hear the call.

The next day, we took two cars to the cabin, where Mom and Dad had decided to scatter Scott's ashes. Greg had his son Matt with him. There were Tom and I, and little Chet; I don't remember who Dad and Mom rode with.

But we got there. Luckily, the current owners weren't in residence. We parked, took photos, walked up Swing Tree Hill. Dipped our hands into the bag of ashes, scattered them up past the Swing Tree, under a huge old oak not far from the barbed wire fence, which had views across the valley behind the cabin. After we were done, photos were taken of us sitting on the bench at the table that Dad had made decades ago.

There is nothing quite like pushing your hand into a bag of the ashes of someone you love. They aren't there . . . it's just the residue of the burning of their physical body. The life, the emotion, the soul had long fled, and what you're touching is merely what is left after flame consumes the physical.

And yet . . . the tactile sensation of the ashes and bits of bone of my loved ones against my living flesh is a sensation that remains with me.

It hurt. I won't lie. Tears were shed as the ashes rained down onto the forest floor. Dad thought Scott would like that, to be among the mountains and trees he'd so loved as a teenager. I have to agree, though in retrospect Hagstone Cove would also have been a good place to scatter his ashes.

Fourteen years later, in 2007, Dad, Greg, my husband Tom, our two kids, and I scattered Mom's ashes in the same spot up at the cabin. Photos were taken. Greg and I whispered to each other that the next time we would see the cabin, it would be when we were scattering Dad's ashes.

That, however, didn't happen. When Chet Cunningham died in March 2017, he left his body to UCSD Medical Center for teaching purposes. I believe it was his way of thanking them for their care of Scott. At any rate, three months later, all the bodies that the medical school had used during that three-month period were cremated together. There was a joint ceremony, scattering those comingled ashes at sea. Greg and I decided not to go to that ceremony. Our goodbyes had already been said.

We had a wake for Dad at the house, about a week after his death, and family and long-time friends came.

To this day, I don't know whether or not it's a good thing, not having a grave to visit. Technically, I don't like graveyards—the earth should be for the living, in my opinion. However, there is something to be said for having a place to visit the dead. Any major cathedral in Europe is testimony to that. And graveyards everywhere have a special feeling about them.

Do I miss having a space to visit them? Yes and no.

It's complicated.

RITUALS FOR REMEMBRANCE

As I mentioned earlier, there was no formal service for Scott that I could go to, nowhere I could grieve publicly, as one does at a funeral service.

I look back now and wish Scott and I had been closer. Part of it was me; not understanding the truth of Scott's life, of being young and selfish, of focusing on my own life to the exclusion of everyone in my family. As well, Scott was an exceptionally private person. He was an old soul, even when he was a child, while I feel my soul is still shiny and new and naïve, and I do not mean that in a superior way.

He loved me. He also tolerated me, laughed at me, sympathized with me, cared for me, put up with me because I was his baby sister.

And I need to be content with that, even as I mourn his loss all these years later.

The few times I am at the ocean alone, I still do a ritual for him. I draw a heart on the wet sand and I put his initials in the middle of the heart. Then I sit and talk to him, listen (sometimes he'll answer), laugh out loud, and send love to him. If the tide is rising, I wait until the heart is wiped clean by the waves. If the tide is going out, I stay as long as I can before saying goodbye and taking my leave.

Whenever I start a fire in the firepit in the backyard, I sit and watch the smoke, watch the flames, see what I can see. I talk to him if I'm alone.

Often, I will take the last bit of wine in my glass and go outside, and under the light of the Moon in Her many phases, I will toss it out into the air, and thank Scott for the blessings he has bestowed upon so many.

In fact, every time I see the Moon, I think of Scott, whether I have wine in a glass for him or not.

I no longer let balloons go due to the wastefulness of it . . . but when I remember, I do like to blow bubbles out into the wind.

Truthfully, I speak to him now more than I ever did in the past. I am also more open to hearing him, knowing when he's near, and I hear him when he responds. There's comfort in that.

At Mom's memorial service, I ordered three Anthurium stems in a vase for the altar at the church. Scott always gave my mother Anthuriums for special occasions, and they quickly became her favorite flower. So Anthuriums, a beautiful Hawai'ian flower, are another way I honor and remember Scott.

There is no right way to grieve. There is no wrong way to grieve. Any ritual you choose to create to remember your beloved dead is just perfect.

I tried to have an Ancestor altar. It got dusty and went uncared-for; not that I didn't care, I just don't think in terms of an altar, though I'm getting better. My home is crowded as it is, and I am not the best of housekeepers.

I use the garden as my Ancestor altar; I think of my grandparents, my parents, and of Scott, every time I'm out there, weeding or watering or harvesting. The scent of star jasmine and orange blossom, the sight of the plumeria, bring them to mind. In the garden, Scott and Dad are close to me. I feel them when weeding the onions and zucchini, when I pick or prune the orange and apple trees. When I watch the birds at the feeder, I feel Mom, her hand on my shoulder.

On a summer evening the bats come out to play, just before it's dark enough to see the first stars. My family is with me then, as well.

There is no right way to honor your beloved dead. If an Ancestor altar works for you, then give it a go. If that's not for you, that's fine. Until I started writing this all down, I had no idea how often my beloved dead are in my thoughts, or how many different ways I honor them.

What I would suggest is, write your own ritual based on what you naturally do. When do you think of your beloved dead? What do you instinctively do? Write it down. Maybe put it in your personal calendar and do something monthly.

While I wish I could write out a beautiful ritual for you, in my heart I know it will be much more meaningful if you create it yourself. Not that you need it, but you have not only my permission but my blessing to go forth and make something beautiful, or simple, or full of joy, as a ritual to remember, and honor, your beloved dead.

CHAPTER TEN

What Came After

SCOTT AND THE CRAFT

I have had people ask me how Scott managed to be "converted" to Wicca. Which is an odd kind of question, and I usually shrug it off; but as I've been reminded, people are curious. They want to know. And in a roundabout way, I can tell you.

Scott was always driven by his need to understand Nature in all Her glory. Questions about the stars led to questions about Nature, which led to more questions. He turned to science for the answers, and when they did not answer all of his questions, he decided to learn what he could to somehow explain and solve these "natural mysteries," as he called them.

In his studies, he eventually found magick, which used the four elements of Nature: Earth, Air, Fire, and Water, plus Spirit. And so his education shifted, again, and he learned and absorbed.

It wasn't a "conversion" in a religious sense. It was more a "turning toward" practices that helped him solve natural mysteries, that helped him feel connected to the world. Scott, who had from his youngest days been enthralled with Nature, finally found a Nature-based religion that spoke to his soul. His research, his studies with others, his innate intellectual curiosity then compelled him to share what he had learned.

He didn't believe one needed a coven to be a good Wiccan. While I know from reading *Whispers of the Moon*, that over his years of study, he was initiated into three or possibly more traditions, he had come to believe one did not need to be initiated. He preferred to use the terms "Wiccan" and "Wicca," instead of "witch" and "witchcraft," as he figured Wicca was "less encumbered" than the word "witch."

Above all, he understood the forces our world was dealing with and how, with the push of a button, nuclear war could decimate the planet. He believed that there was no better time for a Nature-based religion to grow and spread, which is why he wrote *Wicca: A Guide for the Solitary Practitioner.* He actually started that book while he was in basic training for the Navy, in 1977.

More on how he became who he became I cannot say because I do not know, even though I was right there in the same household. But I do know that who he is speaks loud and clear, and kindly, in all of his books.

Probably the book that best reflects him as a Wiccan practitioner is *Cunningham's Book of Shadows.* It was begun in the 1980s. If you could only have one of his books, I'd choose that one. He talks about ritual, he gives recipes for food, an herbal grimoire is included, plus spells . . . it's like everything he's ever written about, but in one book. There are photos of his typed pages and his handwriting. It's probably the most personal book, and for that reason it's my favorite. But then, they're all my favorites.

I wonder who he would have become were he living still in that incarnation. Earth-oriented, definitely. Peace-oriented? Oh yes. I believe he'd have taken on social causes. Our world is badly out of balance; he would have done his utmost to help change that.

Scott as a Mentor

By Dorothy Morrison

I never met Scott Cunningham, but he was my mentor. He mentored hundreds of thousands of other Witches just like me, and in a way that no one else could. He taught us that magic wasn't rocket science. He simplified it in a way we could easily incorporate it into everyday life. But most of all, he reminded us that the world was a magical place, that we—in and of ourselves—were magical, and that we had the power to change our lives. He gave us license to be who we were, while evolving into who we were meant to be.

One of the most important things he taught us, though, was that knowledge shared was power gained, instead of the other way around. That was a game changer, because those who taught the Craft had always been tight-lipped about what they knew. They held it over our heads and kept us coming back in the hope that we might actually learn something useful. By sharing his knowledge, Scott Cunningham created a legacy like no other. We are that legacy. And I shall always be grateful to be a part of it, for what he taught me is largely responsible for the Witch I am today.

While Scott made the Craft more accessible, it wasn't always that way. When I started my journey in the '70s, there was no internet. Occult-related books were scarce, and those available either bordered on absurdity, or were so boring that reading them was akin to watching paint dry. There were no public Wicca 101 classes because metaphysical shops were nearly non-existent. If you traveled off the beaten path, you might be lucky enough to find a botanica. But if you didn't know exactly what you'd come for—or didn't speak Spanish—you could forget about anyone helping you. Finding a teacher was a moot point, because due to personal safety, they'd gone so far underground that an excavator couldn't even dig them up.

It was a hell of a mess for a small-town girl wanting to study the Ancient Arts but giving up was not an option. At least not for me, as I'd witnessed magic firsthand at the feet of some of the folks who'd worked for my parents. There was a tree-whisperer. A horse-whisperer. A woman I watched perform a curse by spitting in both hands and clapping them together. An old man who slipped an endless braid of leather onto my keyring and told me it would always keep me safe. (He was right. I wound up in several traffic accidents that should have killed me but managed to walk away without a scratch.) Of course, I was too young and inexperienced to know it was magic at play. But that didn't matter. The Ancients Arts had its hold on me and refused to ease its grasp until I found my way.

I moved to Houston in 1973 after graduating from high school and got a job downtown. Every day on the way to work, I passed a little white clapboard house with a big "Psychic" sign in front. I really wanted a reading but growing up as a cop's kid had not only taught me the importance of staying alert to my surroundings but made me wary of being cooped up somewhere without a sure-fire escape route. And since I wouldn't have dreamed of getting into a car with someone I didn't know, it occurred to me that walking into a stranger's house—especially in the big city where crime ran rampant—might not be such a good idea.

Still, I couldn't let it go. After fighting with myself for several months, I finally mustered the courage to call the number on the sign and make an appointment. But that did nothing to hush that little voice inside my head. It just babbled right on about danger and axe murderers and serial killers, continuing its torment even as I rang the bell at the psychic's door.

Fortunately, the young woman who opened the door put a stop to all that. Dressed in embroidered jeans and a tie-dyed t-shirt, she was nothing like I'd imagined. She was warm and welcoming, with a casual manner that put me right at ease. And after the reading—which took place at her kitchen table—we sat and talked for an hour or so. The "stranger danger" I'd been so concerned about flew right out the window, and I knew I'd been blessed with a new friend.

In the months that followed, we got together frequently for coffee or just to hang out. So when she invited me to a party the following year—just a casual get-together with some of her closest friends—accepting was a no-brainer. What I didn't know until I got there, though, was that it was an after-coven-meet party. And to say I was horrified when I realized that I was the only person there who wasn't a Witch was putting it lightly. I had no idea what they wanted with me, but I was absolutely certain that it couldn't be good.

Now my mother had always insisted that I could gracefully get out of any situation by remaining calm, collected, and poised. So I took her advice and did my best to make my way to the door. But it wasn't that easy. People kept holding me in conversation. There was nothing I could do without being rude. So I complied, visiting with them as graciously as possible, while inching toward the door.

When the doorknob was nearly within reach, though, another couple stopped me to chat. But unlike the others, they wanted to talk to me about Wicca. I'd never heard that word before and once they explained what it was and what it wasn't, I was both intrigued and relieved. I hadn't been invited to be the evening's ritual sacrifice after all. These folks actually wanted to take me on as a student. It had taken a year for them to scope me out, but I was finally getting what I'd wanted forever. A chance to study the Ancient Arts. And all it took was a simple phone call to a psychic!

I was more than ready to begin my studies, but my teachers subscribed to "Pagan time"—something else I'd never heard of. Of course, I learned what that was in short order. It was just another way of saying, "I'll do it when I feel like it." I have to admit that didn't sit very well with me because I was raised to be on time, instead of inconveniencing others due to my whims. But since I seemed to be the only student who took issue with that—the other students just shrugged when I mentioned it—there was little I could do but wait until my teachers were willing to grace me with their presence.

The day finally came, but instead of a lesson of sorts, I was given a long list of books to read—some of the most boring books ever written—a good number of which didn't seem to have much to do with what I wanted to learn. I got them from the library, anyway, read them all within two weeks, and called my teachers. They were flabbergasted; more to the point, they thought I wasn't telling the truth because none of their other students had ever gotten through the list so quickly. With that in mind, they decided to test me. And even though they asked some of the most obscure, convoluted questions ever phrased, I passed with flying colors.

Truth be told, they didn't know what to do with me exactly. They didn't have a structured lesson plan, and the book list was an effort in keeping me busy while they decided what they wanted to teach and when. So while I aced my test, I didn't get another lesson. Instead, I was told that my attendance at monthly coven meetings, esbats, and sabbats was mandatory. Nothing else.

A couple of months went by. At the following coven meeting, we were all told to practice automatic writing, to keep our daily progress in a journal, and bring it to the next meeting. No instruction, no tips, nothing at all about how I was supposed to practice something I'd never attempted. Not even a starting point. And after checking with the other students, I discovered that we were all in the same boat.

I already knew our teachers didn't have a structured lesson plan, but I was beginning to think they didn't have a plan at all. That they were just coming up with stuff for us to do on the fly. And unfortunately, I was right.

I knew this wasn't going to work for me. But I stuck it out anyway, because I had learned a few things by attending the Esbat and Sabbat rituals. I now had a feel for the God, the Goddess, and the Watchtower

Guardians, and was forming relationships with them. I'd learned how to raise energy in a Circle and was pretty sure I could set up the altar and cast the Circle myself by memory. I was also beginning to see why ritual worship was important, and how performing ritual work as a group could be effective.

I was also learning the mechanics of Wicca as a religion, and its rules and regulations. The "harm none" rule was definitely at play. And even though I had a hard time understanding how anyone could continue to exist on the planet without harming a single person or thing—you can't even eat a tomato without killing it when you pluck it from the vine—I did my best to comply.

What I was not learning was how to bring my personal magical skills to the surface, which was what I really wanted. It was a matter of finding some control over my life, when mundane action failed. This notion was partly due to being raised in the Catholic church where I was taught to pray, leave everything in God's hands, and just have faith that it would all work out for the best. I'd seen firsthand that it didn't always work, even for the most devout. More to the point, though, I saw leaving an issue in someone else's hands—even God's—as more than a little lazy, especially since I'd also been raised with the old adage of "God helps those who help themselves." So I reasoned that if I couldn't help myself by accessing a skill set with which I'd surely been born, I wasn't about to get any help from the God, or the Goddess, or anyone else.

Even so, I continued to attend the coven meetings and rituals, and take "lessons." At the same time, I knew there had to be more to being a Witch than God and Goddess worship, Circle casting, and doing homework without instructions. And if I ever wanted to get to the heart of the problem, I'd have to gather some gumption and ask the right questions. So that's what I did. I asked my teachers.

Their response was both aggravating and patronizing. They reminded me that Wicca was a religion, not some tool to be used to gain personal power, and I'd just have to trust the Goddess to do what was best for me—and for everybody else.

I couldn't believe my ears. I felt like I was back in Catholic school; only this time, they were telling me to leave things in the hands of the Goddess. I wanted to ask them what had happened to "do as you will." I wanted to ask them if the only difference between Wicca and Catholicism was the exchange of a Pope for a Goddess. I wanted to ask them a hundred other things, too. But I didn't. I just stared at them instead.

They went on to say that I was already learning to perform magic by doing my homework. They reminded me that I had, after all, completed the exercises in automatic writing, clairvoyance, prophetic dreaming, and so on to their satisfaction, then all but patted me on the head. My retort was that I had little interest in those subjects, and what I really wanted to learn was how to make things happen. I wanted to learn about herbs and stones and the other ingredients used in magical efforts. I wanted to learn how and when to use them, and how to channel my energy toward a desired result. I should have stopped there, but I didn't. Instead, I pointedly inquired when I might expect the related lessons.

They looked at me like I had three heads. No one spoke for what seemed like forever. And finally, after gaining her composure at my insolence, one of them did. She told me in no uncertain terms that unless I changed my attitude, the answer was, "Maybe never." But even if I did, she said it would be several years before I was ready.

I was done—at least, with them. I felt as if they'd held me at bay for the last four years, something that was likely to continue if I stayed on. So, armed with advice from the Charge of the Goddess—the line that said if I didn't find it within myself, I'd never find it without—I decided that I might not need a teacher after all. Maybe I was supposed to be on my own. I'd just have to be more proactive.

I found a little botanica on the edge of downtown Houston. While there was a language barrier—I only knew enough Spanish to be dangerous—I did find several Anna Riva booklets and some oils that piqued my interest. I hit yard sales and found copies of Sybil Leek's *Diary of a Witch*, Jeanne Rose's *Herbs & Things*, and Zolar's *The Encyclopedia of Ancient and Forbidden Knowledge*. I bought colored votive candles at the grocery store. Then, praying to the Goddess for assistance, I began to experiment.

The 1980s rolled around, and things began to change a bit. A couple of New Age shops opened on the other side of town. And while they carried crystals and other stones, their big business was psychic readings. But since they mainly catered to the "white-light-affirmation-love-fixes-everything" crowd, I soon realized they didn't have what I was looking for.

The '80s also brought changes of a different kind. The bottom dropped out of the Texas oil market, the economy nose-dived, and by 1982, folks were getting laid off right and left. So on a whim, I packed my bags and moved to California.

It was not one of my smarter decisions, as I wound up working three jobs just to keep a roof over my head. I could no longer afford any of the small luxuries to which I'd become accustomed. I couldn't even afford a manicure—something I wasn't willing to do without—so in a last-ditch effort to learn to do my own nails, I applied for a grant and enrolled in nail tech school. In retrospect, that was the best decision I ever made—for that is where my magical journey truly began.

It's been said that magical energy always recognizes its kind, and I was certain that one of the women in my class was a Witch. But because practitioners still didn't feel safe venturing from the broom closet, she wouldn't admit to it, much less speak freely about it. We played a game of cat and mouse for a few months—an innuendo here, a vague reference there—until she felt comfortable enough to finally introduce me to her roommate. A roommate who also happened to be her high priestess.

That introduction opened up a whole new world for me, and on many levels. For one thing, that high priestess's stamp of approval brought an invitation to attend a full moon ritual. And at that ritual, I observed something I'd never seen before, and still find remarkable to this day: Alexandrians, Gardnerians, and Georgians—from neophytes to elders—all circling together. While the ritual was held at the Georgian covenstead, there was no presumption that any of the traditions were, in any way, more viable than the others. They all respected each other and embraced the diversity. But just as important, they all loved and trusted each other. It was obvious that these folks were not only one big, happy family, but thrilled to be together to celebrate the Goddess in the guise of the full moon.

After the ritual, everybody just hung out, munched on refreshments, and socialized. The vibe was much different than that I'd experienced in Houston. And while it was made clear that I was welcome to study any of the traditions represented, there was no pressure. I wound up with an invitation to the next ritual, and left the gathering determined to find out as much about each tradition as possible so I could decide if I wanted to take up my studies again.

What appealed to me about these three groups was that each had a somewhat structured lesson plan and a degree program. And while visiting with different members I'd met, I finally settled on the Georgian trad. For one thing, it was a mixture of Gardnerian and Alexandrian teachings with Celtic leanings. But just as important, it was the most eclectic of the traditions, and I felt that fewer restrictions would give me a chance to spread my wings.

Of course, the Georgians had rules, too—something I discovered in short order. First there was the reading list, which had to be completed before I was given any lessons. Aside from the addition of a few more recently released books, it was much the same as the one given to me in Houston. But the biggest rule—the one that stuck in my craw—was that I was forbidden to work any magic for a year and a day.

Now telling neophytes not to work magic is akin to telling teenagers not to have sex. They're going to do it no matter what you say. And although I nodded my head as if in agreement, I already knew I wasn't going to comply. This time, though, I didn't let my mouth get the best of me. I kept it shut, and simply headed out to buy what I lacked for the reading assignment.

The Insight Bookstore was the only storefront with a metaphysical bent in Bakersfield, California, back then. And while I was delighted that they carried every book on my list, I was even more thrilled to find divine intervention at work in the form of the store clerk. When I placed my books on the counter, she reached around, grabbed two more, and said she thought I needed those, too. The books in question were *Magical Herbalism* and *Earth Power* and there, in that very moment, my whole life changed. I had just been introduced to Scott Cunningham!

◊◊◊

Some folks like to say that Scott Cunningham changed Wicca. But that's not true. Having had formal training himself, in fact, I doubt the thought ever crossed his mind. So traditional, formalized Wicca training with formal initiations continued even after Scott's books were released—and is still in practice today. What Scott did was much more important than that. He gave us tools. He made Wicca accessible. He gave us license to ask questions and expect real answers. But most of all, he not only changed the way we perceived the religion, but general magical practice as well.

Prior to the 1982 release of *Magical Herbalism,* those who taught Wicca were extremely tight-lipped. They only told you what they wanted you to know. And if questioned about something that might reveal any information that didn't fit their criteria, the answer—if one was given at all—was more than ambiguous. Sometimes, it was downright ludicrous.

Spells were extremely hard to come by. If you were even lucky enough to find one, that luck usually ran out as quickly as it came. For invariably, right in the middle of the materials list, was some obscure, but required, spell ingredient. And because we didn't have today's technological tools, finding it meant lots of costly long-distance phone calls, many miles spent traveling store to store, and the patience of Job—while often still coming up empty-handed. And if you actually managed to find that obscure item? You were usually so frazzled that you couldn't even remember why you wanted it to start with.

Scott's books changed all that. For one thing, his work confirmed what I—and thousands of other neophytes—had known all along: that the Craft could neither exist nor survive without magic. That they were partners by design. And if they failed to dance hand in hand, the Craft fell flat. It became little more than another religious sector that left everything up to the Gods while we danced to Their tune.

His books also put information right in our hands. Real information. Information that we could count on and use to further our studies. He gave us magic in the form of spells and charms and served them up in a delectable and easily digestible format. He taught us about the magical properties of herbs, stones, oils, and incense, and gave us comprehensive lists of viable substitutions. Gone were the days of searching out the obscure. We searched our kitchen cabinets instead, because we often already had what we needed, just waiting to be used.

Mere words cannot even begin to express just how important Scott's many substitutions lists were, or what they've meant to me and other magical practitioners across the world. Had it not been for them, I'd still be trying—nearly forty years later—to find what I needed to consecrate my athame. They played a huge role in developing recipes when I started my cottage incense business decades ago, and I still refer to them when creating the products I make today. Those lists changed magical practice forever, and I'll be forever grateful.

As important as those were, though, Scott did much more than that. He reminded us that our world, in and of itself, was a magical place just waiting to be explored. That there was real magic all around us, that everything we saw and touched—even the most inanimate object—had spirit, energy, and life. He taught us that magic was not something to be worn and discarded like an old jacket. Instead, it was practical. It was easily incorporated into our everyday lives. And once done, it would become just as much second nature as flipping a light switch. Moreover, he did so in an easy-going manner that encouraged us to discover the wealth of magic available to us. All we had to do was claim it and use it to better our lives and the lives of those around us.

This changed the way I saw magic and began to work with it. It also changed the way I saw myself. In reading Scott's books, I began to see that I really could change my life. I began to feel as if it was okay for me to create my own magical style, even if it didn't correlate to that of my teachers. I suddenly realized that making mistakes wasn't the end of the world, that the only folks who didn't make mistakes were those who weren't doing anything, and that even if I made a few, I would figure out how to rectify them. Scott Cunningham's work empowered me and not only gave me license to be myself but also gave me license to become the Witch I wanted to be.

Armed with this knowledge, I began a journey of critical thinking. I stripped things down to the bare bones, looked at the big picture, and began to see that some of the things I was being taught didn't add up. Of course, this caused me to ask more questions—not just about magic, but about the reasons we were trained to do some of the things we did. While some of the answers came easily and were reasonable, there were several my teachers couldn't answer. I was dismayed and so were they. They'd simply been teaching us what they'd been taught without ever questioning it.

I'm sure I caused lots of headaches during my training, but I wound up with a few, too. Not long after I'd received my first-degree initiation, my teacher and high priestess decided to move away and leave me in charge of the coven. It obviously was not a job suited to a new initiate, but she promised to continue to train me via snail mail. Everything went well for several months, with me training the neophytes and she training me. Then one day, instead of a new lesson, I received a letter of release. It was the result of a disagreement we'd had due to my independent thinking.

At first, I was crushed. But after a day or two, I decided it was the best thing that ever happened to me. I could finally practice my Craft as I saw fit—this time, without judgment—and prepared to embark upon the solitary path. That didn't work out exactly as I'd planned, though. For when the other coven members discovered I'd been released, they left the coven, too, and begged me to form my own. That meant I'd have to find another teacher to continue my studies; otherwise, I wouldn't be able to initiate my students past first degree—and I wasn't sure I wanted to do that again. But when the teacher I needed showed up unexpectedly a few days later, I had no choice. Divine intervention had come to play. And this time, it had given me a well-needed kick in the butt.

Having my own coven gave me the opportunity to teach the Craft as I thought it should be. I still taught the Georgian tradition as it was laid out, but there were no lessons without detailed instructions. My lessons were type-written and included exercises in magical and mental theory. There were instructions for consecrating and charging ritual tools, as well as practical exercises that outlined how to use them. Best of all, though, I taught my students how to work magic successfully, using items that were easily accessible—something I could never have done without Scott Cunningham's assistance.

By this time, *The Magical Household* was in print and it inspired me just as much as his previous works had. More to the point, though, it started a creative flow in my brain like no other. I began to look at modern conveniences in a whole new light and came to the conclusion that the forerunners of the Craft would never have ground herbs in a mortar and pestle if there had been an easier, quicker, more effective way. Waiting weeks for oils and potions to cure would have gone by the wayside, too, if there had been a way to process them in a matter of hours. So I began to use the blender to grind herbs and make incense. I used the automatic drip coffee maker to brew washes and tonics. And the electric potpourri pot became my go-to for making oils. (I don't know how Scott would have felt about all that, but I think it would have made him smile.)

Over the years, I waited for Scott's new books with bated breath, excited to see what treasures he had in store for me. This was especially true after an unexpected move in 1990 landed me in the Missouri Bible belt—Scott provided me with a sense of camaraderie in a place where it was still not safe to be out of the broom closet. It was so conservative there, in fact, that someone who'd seen my crystals actually reported us to Child Protective Services—something that fortunately was resolved after one visit. But for someone who'd had her own coven and been somewhat free to express herself, it was like a punch in the gut.

Shortly after, though, I was introduced to PODSnet—a Pagan networking BBS system—that connected Pagans worldwide. That connection gave me a sense of freedom again, even though it was over a dial-up modem. I was not only able to meet others of a like mind but also share spells and rituals and exchange information. And I saw Scott's hand in that, too, as much of what we shared and the opinions we'd formed had obviously come from reading his books. I met people—some in the same town in which I was living—formed friendships and took on new students. The situation became livable again, and I breathed a little easier.

The internet arrived a few years later, and the information network exploded. Pagan websites with forums and occult-related groups sprang up. While online shopping wasn't the norm yet, metaphysical storefronts began to appear on streets everywhere. And as the years rolled by, those stores began to offer classes. Not just general classes about herbs and stones and tarot, but Wicca 101 classes—the latter of which I never thought I'd see.

I wish Scott had lived to see those Wicca 101 classes, as his courage in sharing information and making it accessible was largely responsible for their birth. I wish he'd lived to see the impact he had on Wicca, on Paganism, and on magical practitioners across the globe. I wish he'd known just how much we loved him, how many lives he changed, and how valuable he was to all of us. But most of all, I wish he'd known that, to a large degree, he shaped a young, small-town girl from Texas into the Witch she is today. I hope I've made him proud.

CHAPTER ELEVEN

What Lives On

LEGACY

Several events stand out in my mind after Scott's death, two of which made me hyper-aware of Scott's impact on the world.

The first one? My husband Tom Ashworth was the artistic director for Nevada Shakespeare in the Park in Henderson, Nevada, from 1986 to 1996. In 1995, he directed *Macbeth*. As a part of the set design, he created a partial pentagram painted on the stage floor, which the three witches of *Macbeth* would finish off in action during the play.

There were other symbols painted onto the stage floor. I don't remember which ones he used, but he told me he had chosen them from one of Scott's books. I felt it honored Scott, in so many different ways.

At every Shakespeare in the Park production at that time, the local high school kids came out in droves, because the play they were reading in English Lit was whatever play Nevada Shakespeare was doing. Synergy, right? (In 1993, when we did *Romeo and Juliet*, we had over 5,000 people per show, sitting on blankets. It was amazing.)

So, there we were. Opening night of *Macbeth,* and everything went fine. Afterward, I'm behind the stage with the actors and the hubby and my not-quite-five-year-old who played Fleance, and my almost-two-year-old. A bunch of these high school kids came back (we were in Green Valley Park, before the amphitheater had been built) and they were talking with Tom. They asked questions, he answered, and pointed toward me . . . and before I knew what was happening, I had about a dozen teenagers falling at my feet, just because I was Scott Cunningham's sister.

I've never been more flustered. The hero worship energy coming from those kids bombarded me as much as their gabbled questions. I now know that being empathic, their energy really did "hit" me, and not in a good way; but back then I was much less self-aware.

Luckily, my youngest, who had been with friends up to this point, started crying and needing me, so I was able to escape with grace. But that episode shook me. It gave me a strange insight to what it must be like for an actor, suddenly famous. Or a singer who hits it big and goes out in public for the first time without being aware of what is about to happen to them. It was on quite a minor scale, and yet, it shut me down. It made me aware that, while I could not and would not change a thing about being Scott's sister, perhaps that fact would be something that should not be tossed about in casual conversation.

The second, far less pleasant, episode happened at my corporate job that same year. This woman I knew in passing asked about the AIDS bracelet I wore, and I told her a little about Scott, who he was, how he was missed.

She then basically attacked me for having Scott as a brother. She shredded his stance on Wicca and magick, declared he had gone to hell because of his beliefs (not to mention for being a homosexual). She lambasted me for loving him. She was very like the Christian Far-Right that is holding this country hostage right now. Another reason I started being extremely cautious about sharing my relationship to Scott.

Later, someone accused me of bragging and making myself more important because of the relationship. Oh, and let's not forget those people who dismissed Scott as a lightweight, traitor, spiller of secrets, untalented, take your pick of derisive words. After that, I became—not paranoid, no, but extremely careful about when, and to whom, I spoke of Scott and me being siblings.

The third event was as unpleasant, in a totally different way, as the event at my workplace. Twenty years after Scott's death, I went to a San Carlos neighborhood reunion. One of our old neighbors (a man a couple years older than me) recognized me by my name tag and gave me a big hug. Then he proceeded to apologize for being a part of a group who bullied Scott in junior high, so very long ago. He was Scott's age, or maybe a year or so either way.

That is a wound inside me that still hasn't healed. I have wondered ever since if, or rather how much, Scott was bullied in school. When Greg read this part of the book in an early iteration, he said, "Ask me about the fight." So I did. Here's what Greg said.

"We were in school at Pershing Jr. High, and we all got out at the same time. Scott was in seventh grade; I was in ninth grade. We didn't normally walk home together.

"One time, I came around the corner and saw a circle of kids surrounding another kid. There wasn't much talk, just a lot of pushing and shoving. I pushed my way toward them and then realized Scott was the kid in the center of the circle.

"I pushed through the circle, put my hand on Scott's back, and pushed him through the other side, and we walked home. We didn't discuss it. He didn't say thank you. I didn't say you're welcome. We just walked home."

I don't know if this was the first time he was bullied. I don't know if either of them ever told my parents, but I do know that I never heard a thing about it at home. That he went through that without a word to anyone outside of the incident Greg witnessed hurts my heart. I still don't know what to do with it. It doesn't fit into the narrative that I have in my head and heart of Scott, and yet, it happened.

Have I mentioned that my branch of Cunninghams didn't talk about important stuff? This would be filed under that category. Except it has been brought to my attention that here I am, talking about this stuff. Because yes, it's important.

A fourth episode that showed me how much Scott impacted the world happened when I went to that metaphysical store on Lankershim Boulevard, the one where I fell in love with incense. Well, they carried Scott's books. When the owner saw me stroking the spine of his books (I always do when I see them in a physical bookstore—it's one way I say "hi" to Scott), she came over and asked me if I'd read his work before. I blurted out that I was Scott's sister, and she hugged me. Then she invited me to a private, but open, Samhain ritual happening later that month. Pure acceptance, no judgment. Until she gave me that, I didn't realize how much I needed it.

It has taken me a long time to share openly about having Scott as my brother, much less about being a solitary practitioner myself, because for the longest time I never knew what kind of reaction I would get. Some people I felt safe to confide in; at other times, it was best to keep silent.

I'm sharing now because who he was has informed who I am becoming. I want to share him, the boy and man I knew, because I'm the only one who can. It wasn't time for me to be open about this any earlier than right now.

Scott was all about being true to who you are. If only bits of his books work for you, and bits of other people's books work for you, then go, you! You're educating yourself. You're seeking answers. Finding what works for you was always at the heart of what Scott had to offer. Offering to everyone the knowledge he had was paramount. That's who he was, at heart. What you did with that knowledge was up to you.

He didn't believe that you had to be in a coven in order to learn about magick, or about Wicca. He most definitely didn't believe in the "One True Way" to be a witch or a Wiccan.

Writing his books was a way for Scott to provide for others, those who did not have the teachers or the advantages that he had. This responsibility weighed on him, to the point that the last three years of his life he pushed himself, hard, to get books completed before he couldn't anymore.

I recently discovered some folks have said his books were tossed together, he had no training of any sort, and he just made stuff up out of whole cloth. To me, that means they never read his work. And you know what? That's fine. Opinions. Everyone has them.

Did he want to open up Wicca for everyone? Yes. Did he do so? In my opinion, yes, he did. Did he get death threats from the Wiccan and occult communities for doing so? Yes, he did. Scott mentioned it to me once and never mentioned it again, though Dad discussed it with me a couple of times.

So no, not everyone loves Scott, or his books. Which is exactly how it should be. One size does not fit all, no matter what anyone says.

We are not meant to be shoved into a mold and all come out the same. It's impossible. Humanity is too curious, too egocentric at times to want to be like everyone else. Our individuality should be celebrated and enjoyed. We should all be accepted as we are, for who we are.

At the same time, we all need a place to belong. No one enjoys feeling left out, feeling abandoned, or feeling like no one can possibly understand who they are or what they're going through. Which is why for many, belonging to a coven is so important. And anyone who swears they have the One True Way to be a witch, or a Wiccan, is someone you should probably run away from.

I believe that giving each other grace, and being kind, is the way to go. I believe that Scott also ascribed to that motto. I have seen him impact more people than he ever imagined he would; how his work has resonated across the world.

Be kind. Be who you are. Don't force yourself to be someone else's idea of who you should be. Walk the path that feels right to you. It may take time; there are many paths out there, including ones that haven't been created yet.

Scott always walked the path he felt was the right one for him. He was true to himself, and encouraged those he interacted with to do the same.

Just remember to be true to your own soul. It's really that simple.

Gratitude: Scott Cunningham Remembered

By Stephanie Rose Bird

We all have our liaison, through magickal source books that serve as a portal to other worlds and the otherworldly. Whether metaphysical fiction, or what was once called alternative spirituality, and what we now appreciate as earth-based spirituality, these books help transform our way of thinking.

For a child of the '70s who fully stepped into her magickal witch's boots in the '90s, one of those important guides was Scott Cunningham. He had a warm, inviting tone and a way of making the world of Wicca, including magical herbs (my love), metallurgy, crystals, stones, and incense, from around the world, accessible and approachable. One of my well-worn books that I must have on my bookshelf is *Wicca: A Guide for the Solitary Practitioner*, another is *Cunningham's Encyclopedia of Magical Herbs*, not to mention *The Magical Household*.

Over the years I have referred to Cunningham's works in my practice. As with so many books of those times, I scoured his works for hints or information from or about the African Diaspora. That connection I sought, by and large, was sketchy or not to be found. Rather than get angry, I took it as a call to action. I eventually pulled away from my easel and palette long enough to communicate what I needed on paper with pen. I believed others who looked like me, and some who do not, were interested in having the spirituality and healing ways of the

African Diaspora be accessible too. I became an author inspired by what I read and, perhaps as importantly, what I did not. Scott Cunningham remains a pivotal figure and for that he will always be remembered.

With gratitude and in remembrance of the trailblazer, Scott Cunningham.

SCOTT TODAY—AND TOMORROW

If Scott were alive, I imagine he would thoroughly utilize all the electronic tools now available to us to spread his message of honoring Mother Earth, his message that we are all magick and that we all are capable of magick.

I believe he'd have continued his push on saving the environment; he recycled before it was the thing to do, first by convincing Dad to save newspapers for the Boy Scouts that came around on a monthly basis. They recycled newspapers for money for their troop, which was good enough for Dad to sign onto that plan. Scott, on his own, recycled Dad's huge stash of coke cans and while I was dancing, my sixteen-ounce bottles of Diet Dr. Pepper.

Scott might even have organized a group of his own, a school of sorts based on his books, although he shied away from even thinking about that when he was in his thirties. He didn't want the responsibility of leading people, as he'd seen how divisive different groups could become, and found all the infighting tiresome. It is my belief, however, that time, and his friends, might have changed his mind.

He certainly wouldn't have stopped learning. He'd have enjoyed meeting today's authors and practitioners; he would have, I am certain, studied with those that caught at his imagination. He would have been initiated into new paths, he would have embraced his sexuality in this new environment, and he might even have written books on different paths, as his own studies deepened.

The thing is no one person or religion has a monopoly on the path to enlightenment. Let me say that again. *No one person or religion has a monopoly on the path to enlightenment.* There is nothing wrong with trying all paths that may speak to you, and I encourage you to do so.

My goal in writing this book is to extend Scott's message, and especially the message that was not ever spoken out loud and that is, there is room in the Pagan/Wiccan/witchcraft world for everyone. Every marginalized group? He would open this door to you.

Correction. He *has* opened this door to you.

Every person, no matter the color of their skin, is welcome. Every person, no matter what their sexuality or gender identity may be, is welcome. Every person, no matter what their disability, is welcome.

Dad expected Scott's books to sell another ten to fifteen years after his death. The reason they continue to sell well, thirty years on, is that Scott did not place limits on who should have access to the knowledge he shared. That, after all, is why he shared it, so those who are marginalized could have access to knowledge that otherwise would be hidden from them.

Every person who has read his books and continued on and learned more from other resources has carried on Scott's message.

Every person who has thanked the tree for its fruit or its shade has carried on Scott's message.

Every person who points another to Scott's work has carried on his message. Even those people who decry Scott as a lightweight, a fluffy bunny, unoriginal and lacking in Wiccan/witchcraft training, thus leading people to seek out Scott's work to see for themselves, has carried on his message.

To all of you, I believe he would say, without reservation, a heartfelt thanks.

Thank you all for sharing his work so widely.

Thank you.

Scott's Impact

By Michelle Welch

Scott Cunningham may very well be the voice that gave rise to generation after generation's sustained education of all things magical. I own three thriving metaphysical stores and I can unequivocally state that Scott Cunningham's books not only sell out almost instantly but are also requested or recommended on a daily basis. Ahead of his time, Cunningham is still providing us with the answers to which we seek direction. I wish I had known Scott Cunningham, this magical gift to the publishing industry, but I am grateful to know his sister. More people like Scott and Christine are needed in the world today.

I devour three to five books weekly, so I humbly consider myself a very good source of the books on the market in the "New Age" (for lack of a better word) genre. I have always read a lot. I remember having a flashlight under the covers when I was little because I always wanted to read. I say all this to add that I was not allowed to read any New Age, metaphysical, or "witchy" books growing up, but I sure have made up for it, and I started with Scott's books. He had a way of writing that seemed to anticipate every question I had, and he never shoved an opinion down my throat. Yes, he wrote with authority and confidence, yet his books allowed me the room to formulate my own conclusions on how to best integrate his wisdom into my life and practices.

Another thing that continues to impress me about Scott's writing is that I read his books over and over. Despite all the books that have been published in recent years, Scott Cunningham's books live on as staples needed for almost every area of a metaphysical practice. We tell the thousands of people that come through our doors at SoulTopia, LLC, that Scott Cunningham books are beginner to advanced. It is very rare, actually almost impossible, for an author to successfully appeal to such a broad audience, yet Scott's writing did just that.

I had the pleasure of meeting his sister Christine a few years ago. I found her delightful and subsequently ordered her book, *Wear the Pearls and Other Bits of Wisdom*. At the time of our meeting, she made absolutely no mention of her famous brother Scott. When I found out later in the weekend that she was Scott's sister, I was even more impressed by this remarkable woman and author. Christine is a steady, grounded woman and brilliant author in her own right. I am proud to call her friend. I recently wrote a book that included looking at spirit guides and ascended masters in a broader way than perhaps we have considered. I know without a doubt that Scott Cunningham in spirit serves as a guide and ascended master to me when I am writing. I am sure he does for many. I also know without a doubt that Christine serves as a spirit guide (yes, in human form) to me. She is a wise teacher, writer, lecturer, friend, and mentor to many. Scott and Christine both will continue to help not only individuals, but publishers, achieve spiritual goals, and for that I have immense gratitude.

CHAPTER TWELVE

Letters, Tarot, Endings

CHRISTMAS LETTERS

Here are the excerpts about Scott from the Christmas letters my parents would send each year. Please note: I have shared them as they were written, without any edits. My comments (if any) are in parentheses. Oh, and Dad wrote every Christmas letter.

1957: "Scotty is 1½ this Christmas. He's learning to say a few words, but is still basically a pointer, grunter, and cryer. He has a sly little smile and a giggly laugh that keep his parents broken up most of the time. He's a chair pusher, a stander on sofas, a mommy-purse rustler, and a dabbler in the washing. He also has an incredible appetite and gets very demanding when there's food around. Can't get that little bear filled up."

1959: ". . . we have invested in a new spinet piano for the family . . . Scotty would like to take lessons too, he is a real 'me too' kid, but he's a bit too young at 3½."

1960: "Scotty—the middle sized tiger is about 4½ now, and starting to reach out in all sorts of ways. He is shedding his shyness and becoming more aggressive and independent and inventive. Wishes he could go to school too, or at least have someone to play with when Greg is gone. 'What can I do?' is a typical question for Scotty. Loves small animals and flowers and sunsets. Rosie is sure he is going to be the poet. He's a collector of small bugs, frogs, butterflys and crickets. Careful of that pocket!"

1961: "Scotty—the 5½ year-old bouncer is still heading toward the poetry corner. He is now proudly in kindergarten and loving every minute of it. Scotty is shedding his shell and charging toward more independence. He is the more sensitive of the boys. Enjoys playing with his little sister, coloring, the big outdoors sandbox, and his record player. New found outlet is tempera painting, it washes out easily!"

1962: "Scotty, age six, is in the first grade, and 'at last' learning to read and write. He loves it. Have a brother who is two years ahead of him in everything sometimes is just too much, but he is coming into his own now. He seemed to be born with perfect pitch and a good natural sense of rhythm and feeling for music, so we started him on piano lessons, and started Greg again too, this fall. This time they have a fine teacher and she has their complete devotion. They do their practicing as soon as they get up in the morning."

1964: "Scott, 8, third grade. He is in Cubs now that he is 'of age,' and is devouring the material. Scott came up with a 95% in the piano auditions in June and savored the sweet triumph of placing higher than his brother. His interests center on the artistic—he loves to make pictures and puppet shows and he has been making Disneyland-type rides for about five months. He has little interest yet in sports."

1965: "Scott, now a growing 9 years, is a Cub Scout, sings in the junior choir at church and is very interested in animals, rocks and everything that has to do with the ocean. Scott learned to swim this year after taking lessons. He's starting to spend more time reading and discovering books. Scott thinks he might want to be a marine biologist someday. He works at his piano lessons every day before going to school."

1966: "Scotty, now 10½. An eater. He has reached that glorious age of the empty plate, the empty stomach, the empty stare and the 'hungries' after every meal. Scheduled for a three-inch growth (height) this year, he is also a Cub Scout, singer in church Jr. Choir, and attender at 5th grade in school. Current craze is making monster machines, spook houses, 'rides of all sorts,' paper cutouts and figures. Loves to put on 'shows', sells pinecones and apricots to our neighbors, and may wind up being another Barnum or Disney. That's our Scotty!" (Note: The pinecones came from our newly acquired cabin in the Laguna Mountains.)

1968: "Scott, 12, is in the 7th grade and enjoying junior high. He has taken up piano lessons again, after a three-year break. He and Christine have an exceptionally fine teacher, and they're doing well. You should see Scott's collection of seashells. He has wooden drawer cases for them and has them all set on cotton and labeled with the Latin and common name. Scott is interested in all phases of the ocean and in electronics." (Note: My dad made the wooden case with about fifteen drawers in it, slightly taller than your normal two-drawer file cabinet.)

1969: "Scott is 13, in the eighth grade and still adds to his shell collection. He has hundreds and knows them by their Latin and common names. Wants to go to Hawaii and the great Barrier Reef by Australia to get more! He has a fine touch on the piano and is taking lessons from a teacher who performs nightly. His teacher wants to get him into a 'group.' Scott hopes to get a small electric organ."

1970: "Scott has grown taller than his mom and dad this past year and at 14 is stretching up toward big brother. His interests lean toward records, stagecraft and large quantities of food and sleep." (Note: By "records," Dad meant show tunes and movie scores.)

1971: "Scott is closing in on 16 and is in a play downtown. He's in *Taming of the Shrew*, an all-teen-age cast and loving it. Scott has taken a renewed interest in the piano and pounds it every day. He's also taking ice skating lessons and having fun his sophomore year in high school." (I had no idea he took ice skating lessons. Nor do I know why Dad got Scott's age wrong. He'd have been solidly fifteen here.)

1972: "Scott, 15, struck out into drama, acting at a community theater downtown in a role in *Taming of the Shrew*. They gave nine performances including one 'road trip' at another town." (Note: I do not know why my dad repeated the Shrew comment from the previous year. I don't think they did that production two years in a row. Plus, he'd have been sixteen here.)

1973: "On December 26, Scott and Rosie will fly to Mexico City for eight days. They will be going as part of our chancel choir which has been invited to take part in the celebration of the centennial of the founding of the Methodist Church in Mexico. Besides the singing there will be planned sightseeing, touring and unforgettable fellowship. We're polishing dthems* like mad. Rosie started a course in conversational Spanish and took it for three months." (*No clue—probably anthems.)

1973 continued: "Scott's a high school Senior, has applied to go to San Diego State University. He's going to major in drama and journalism. He has been studying piano with a professor at the college since last spring. He really enjoys it. He's performing in a dance review at high school for three days and co-directing a production of 'Spoon River Anthology' to go on the boards in January."

1974: "Scott is finishing his first semester at San Diego State University, is still interested in drama, journalism, and writing. He's taking whatever courses he can get into, 33,000 students there. He's now writing a newspaper humor column for several auto dealers and is selling it. Still plays the piano, and does taxi work for mom and sis." (Note: He drove me many times to my ballet classes and rehearsals.)

1975: "Scott is a sophomore at San Diego State and currently an English major. He thought about majoring in German but changed his mind and thinks he may want to write. In June he had Type A hepatitis, the milder kind. He spent a month in bed. It wasn't the best summer for him. He's going to school full time and feeling well, except for tiredness."

1976: "Scott, 20, is a junior at San Diego State majoring in English and he enjoys writing. He's been selling a few articles to trade journals about trucks. He worked six months at Sea World and is job hunting."

1977: "Scott is working at an extended day-care center, says he really loves it, and is writing too. He's doing articles for trade magazines and trying fiction in the science fiction field. He also goes to the writer's workshop meetings with his dad."

1978: "Scott has turned back to the typewriter. He's working in the home office now with a desk and typewriter of his own and a dozen freelance projects concentrating on nonfiction in the trucking field, but branching out into other forms of articles and his writing includes work on a novel. He has his own apartment but comes in every day to work." (Note: Scott and I had moved into the apartment at 4349 Orange Avenue soon after I graduated from high school a half-year early in January 1978.)

1979: "Scott does temporary typing assignments in between his writing work and half his income is from freelance writing. He has written and sold two short novels and a book on herbs and sells lots of articles on trucks for trade magazines."

1980: "Scott continues his writing. He's taken over the car and truck columns from Chet, and is also writing short novels [. . .] He's selling them and learning as he goes."

1981: "Scott continues writing, doing automotive and truck columns and short novels."

1982: "Scott found out last month that he has Burkitt's disease; cancer of the lymph nodes. This has a high recovery rate and we're full of optimism. He's not incapacitated and is responding well to treatment. Scott continues to write and publish."

1983: "Scott is in San Diego, writing non-fiction books and working at word processing in an office." (Note: A lot of Dad's letter this year was around his TRS-80, his very first computer. The rest of us got short shrift, which makes me laugh now.)

1984: "Our kids are all doing fine, Scott is selling non-fiction books, Chris is in Hollywood struggling to get into Show Business, and Greg is here in town and working on the largest Cable TV firm in the world."

1985: "Scott is writing novels, novelizations and non-fiction books about herbs and magick and lives in San Diego."

1986: "Scott is in town here freelance writing in occult books. Scott just finished his first video. It's a 40 minute VCR tape that will be sold through his publisher. He's quite proud of it. We'll see it soon."

1987: "Son Scott is working hard as a selling writer, concentrating on magical, herb and occult books, and making a name for himself. He's been on a national TV talk show, and makes speaking engagements around the country, teaches classes and writes."

1989: "Scott lives in San Diego and continues to sell books he writes about magick and herbalism."

1991: "Scott is here in town and writing books. He's just finished one on Hawaii."

1993: "As you may know, our youngest son, Scott died in April from a series of complicated problems. We miss him. He was a well-known author in the occult, mystic and 'New Wave' fields. He has 15 books on the shelves. Some have been selling for 10 years. All will continue to sell for another 15 or 20 years." (Note: Dad most likely meant New Age and not New Wave. Scott's books are still selling quite well as of this writing; all of them are still in print.)

Scott Cunningham's Roots

by Beverly Frable

There are many people who feel a connection with nature, yet there are few who seem to have nature embedded in every cell of their body. Scott was the latter. His writings, for me, seemed to be the voice of the trees, the plants, and all of their magical energies.

Scott's abilities to see the magic in nature opened doors to understanding the true power that existed in the world around us. Through his eyes, I learned that leaves spoke to me, especially when the wind created opportunities for them to express their sounds or movements.

My connection to Scott's words became more deeply rooted (pun intended) when I read one of his more famous quotes about trees, from his book *Earth Power*:

> Trees have from time immemorial been closely associated with magic. These stout members of the vegetable kingdom may stand for as long as a thousand years, and tower far above our mortal heads. As such they are symbols and keepers of unlimited power, longevity, and timelessness. An untouched forest, studded with trees of all ages, sizes and types, is more than a mysterious, magical place—it is one of the energy reservoirs of nature. Within its boundaries stand ancient and new sentinels, guardians of the universal force which has manifested on the Earth.

He was ahead of his time. Science is only now "discovering" how trees form communities, sharing resources and supporting the weaker trees by providing extra nourishment, if needed. In fact, trees have been shown to keep stumps alive so that the stump's extensive root systems can be used as a part of a communication network. It's also now been proven that trees avoid infringing on the territory of other trees in their area, and that trees are capable of establishing warning systems to ward off predatory insects. All of these scientific findings occurred well after Scott recognized trees as being "energy reservoirs of nature."

Another one of Scott's works that impacted my life was one that spoke to the spiritual and cultural lessons of Hawaii: his book *Hawaiian Magic & Spirituality*. This book offered insights not understood by many outside Hawaii's indigenous people, detailing spiritual beliefs tied to nature and the elements dating back to many years prior to the arrival of Christianity. Once again, he demonstrated an understanding and depth that surpassed others, especially considering his young age.

How did Scott know what he knew? Was it intuitive, learned . . . or a combination of both? I've been in awe of his wisdom for years. Now we all have an opportunity to learn more about Scott, thanks to Christine's sharing of personal insights and experiences. Over my years of knowing Christine, she's shared many stories of her childhood with Scott. I was absolutely thrilled to learn that she was writing a book about him to share with the world. Not only is gaining insight into Scott, the person, one of the things that most excites me about Christine's book, I also believe it's important to document the life of someone who was a true trailblazer, someone who had such a heightened understanding and relationship with nature. This book is a gift to our world.

Thanks to Christine, future generations will now get to know Scott, too. His work will continue to live on, and his life will continue to make a difference. This fills me with hope for the future. It very well may open doors for others so that they, too, gain a better understanding of our place in the world and our connections to all that lives.

Scott Cunningham through a Tarot Lens

By Jaymi Elford

Scott Cunningham was instrumental during the beginning phases of my witchy path through the early 2000s. His outlook on the five elements helped pave the way for how I ended up reading tarot! So, I feel it's a fitting tribute to bring my tarot path around to talk about his tarot soul path cards.

This is a technique taught to me by innovative tarot authority, Mary K. Greer. In this technique, she combines numerology and the twenty-two Major Arcana cards into an interesting introspective way to examine how you fit into the cards.

Your "soul path" cards are between one to three cards that show the energies surrounding you on the date you were born. They are a guiding archetype for what you were born to become. They have a big influence on how you interact with the world and those in it. Who you are and how you navigate life can be influenced by these cards. My personal soul cards speak to who I am and what I've chosen to do in life. You use the day, month, and year you were born to calculate which Major Arcana cards are your soul cards.

In this article, we'll do a deep dive to perform this process and examine what his cards are and how the energies may have influenced his life and his pagan path.

Calculating this number requires you to have your birthday, a calculator, and some familiarity with the twenty-two Major Arcana cards. We use the number one through twenty-two, where the number twenty-two becomes The Fool's card. We don't want to leave the first step out from the experience they can lend to our lives.

Scott Cunningham was born on June 27, 1956. We write this down as:

Day: 27
Month: 06
Year: 1956

Adding this up, we get 1989 as the final number.

However, we don't stop there. We need to reduce this number to something between one and twenty-two. So, we add each of the four numbers in 1989 to get a final number of twenty-seven. Since twenty-seven doesn't fit within our range, we reduce it down further by adding two and seven together to get nine.

In Scott's case, he has a single soul path card of nine. In a tarot deck, this card represents The Hermit.

While many people believe The Hermit is about moving through life alone and solo, this most certainly isn't the case. Yes, the image on the card shows an elder person (often male perceived) wearing a gray cloak and standing high atop a mountainside. The figure is often holding a staff in one hand while the other arm reaches out with a lantern. A six-pointed star shines forth from this. In the Rider Waite Smith deck, we see very little ground. The sky is bright blue, giving The Hermit a fantastic backdrop for their light to shine far out into the distance. It's this light that draws many to climb the mountain that our tarot Hermit stands on. And when the people arrive, they are treated to the knowledge and wisdom the Hermit has gained from the years of transforming their practice into something workable and sharable.

People with Hermit soul path cards are seekers. They want to know all about the topic that appears deep in their heart, mind, and spirit. In many cases, those born under The Hermit have a curious nature about spiritual pursuits. Therefore, Hermits think a lot and read and research best practices before they share what they know. With all the books Scott Cunningham wrote, we can see that he was a spiritual seeker. It's like he wanted to know the truth of existence as well as how to make a spiritual path using the tools of the Earth right at our fingers. Early on, Scott studied many traditions and was initiated into three different traditions. (*Whispers of the Moon* by deTraci Regula and David Harrington. Llewellyn, 1997.)

All this knowledge gained and practices done would give Scott a good grounding in developing his own practices and interpreting them for others. So, of course, he would start working on his own variants, on his own terms, to record his experiments and successes on paper.

Every time he would tell someone about his ideas, they would get interested as well. So, he would go back to his journals, through the work he did to start teaching and sharing it. Having come from a family of authors, he would choose the written word as his preferred delivery method of getting his ideas to as many people as he could.

Hermits, being the masters of their own internal wisdom, can also become very successful at what they do. Scott definitely shows us this leadership quality with his incredible body of work on various metaphysical topics. He kept his solitude and silence when he needed to. But in the end, as every other Hermit in history has done before him, he picked up the lantern to bring those who noticed to him. He shared what he knew with the world and became a mentor to many aspiring witches.

Hermits don't typically turn their back on society for very long. They do retreat, learn and harness their power, but many come back to share their wisdom. We see it throughout many great religious texts and pop culture archetypes. Scott had his solitary witch path going for many years. He may not have set out to become a mentor, but his way with words and his approach was accessible to all who read his books. His solitary path helped pave the way for many others to replicate his own process from the words he wrote and to continue repeating their brand of witchcraft sabbat after sabbat.

It's true that he may have preferred to be alone, working with his tools, and practicing his beliefs. But it was his love for the craft and his ability to write his passion on the page that we have been graced with his words and his views on so many metaphysical topics from ritual to crystals and more. Thank you for your illumination, Scott. I would not be where I am without having read and studied your work.

In writing this piece, I find it also fitting that Christine chose to tell me her soul cards. They are The Star and Strength. I see much strength in her desire to share Scott's personal journey with others, and her ability to elevate the star on The Hermit card out through the world with this work.

Scott's Legacy Tarot Spread

By Ethony Dawn

Like many modern witches, I have a number of Scott Cunningham books on my shelf. They're read and re-read, borrowed out and referenced over the years. Scott brought a lot of important information to my life and my Craft is better for it. He's a name I say often when it comes to recommendations for those new to the Craft. I feel it's important to remember the people who really brought a sense of modernization mixed with tradition to the witch's craft. We would not be where we are today if it weren't for authors and souls like Scott. I created this tarot spread for Scott to thank him in spirit for being the inspiration for the prompts.

Whether you desire to write books and reach millions as Scott did, or if your legacy is more local, we all leave something behind. So light a candle, a representation of your own inner flame and spirit; gather your favorite tarot deck, and enjoy this tarot spread.

Spirit of Legacy Tarot Spread

1. **Wonder**—How can I reinvigorate my sense of joy?
2. **Legacy**—What is my soul here to leave behind?
3. **Curiosity**—Where should I start to explore?
4. **Tradition**—What traditions should I keep and pass on?
5. **Evolution**—What in my practice requires development and change?

WRAPPING IT UP

I don't know how to end this book. I wish I did. My cat Zaphod is asleep on the corner of my desk, in a box. He's snoring. My husband is sorting his paints in the dining room, in preparation for going to work in *Much Ado About Nothing* at Denver Center Theater in Denver, Colorado. He leaves in two weeks.

It's been in the upper nineties, temperature-wise, for several days. People are tired of COVID; they're tired of politics even as they gear up for mid-terms in November. In the past two weeks alone, wildfires and flooding have devastated different areas of the country. At times, it feels like the culture of hate is winning.

My pupdog Whimsy is getting over having two teeth extracted a week ago today. One son is at work; the other is writing in his bedroom. It's hot in the house because the peak time period for electricity usage is between four and eight in the evening, which means they charge you up the wazoo for wattage and who can afford to run the air conditioner?

I'm going into my third year of working from home; only now I'm in my day job's office three days a week. COVID-19 ran through our family at the end of June 2022, and while everyone has mostly recovered, I find I am not back to normal quite yet.

Tom and I have been slowly turning our huge backyard into a Victory garden. The fig tree and the orange tree that we planted in the spring of 2021 are still alive and the fig looks like it will bear fruit this fall. Unfortunately, our two avocado trees that we planted in 2020 didn't survive the 114° heat in August of that year.

The sunflowers are amazingly beautiful this year, and I've been documenting them on Instagram. Earlier this year we planted zucchini, cucumber, peppers, onions, celery; the kale from last summer is still growing strong and getting tall. Harvesting fresh veggies and making salads with them are a joy. Tom created a watering system out of PVC pipe and it's working wonders. Who knew that watering was the secret to gardening? Only now, because of the third year of drought we're in, which came hard on the heels of a six-year drought interrupted by two fairly normal rain years, we are only allowed to water once a week so soon our garden will be a memory.

Tom and Whimsy and I have been walking the foothills of Simi Valley, areas we wouldn't have known to look for in years past but at least we're getting exercise. We're finding places we can walk that aren't inhabited by anything but bunnies and birds, butterflies and bees. The quiet back in the hills is a luxury we don't get too often.

We hit the beach as often as we can, as early in the day as we can to avoid the crowds and enjoy the marine layer.

Is it wrong to be grateful that my parents and Scott are gone and didn't have to deal with this pandemic? If it is, I'm okay with that. To have them to worry about during this time is not my idea of fun, and my heart is with those who are in that position.

I don't know how to end this book.

Scott was a complicated person, as most of us are. He was highly intelligent, highly motivated. He did that first book, *Magical Herbalism,* on his typewriter. He did the bibliography by hand first and the appendix via typewriter, and the internet did not yet exist. The man had mental stamina.

He stood a little over six feet, broad-shouldered, with brown hair and kind blue eyes. He was neither thin nor fat, but he was definitely sturdy. Sometimes he had a mustache; sometimes he did not. His hair started thinning early, thanks to heredity.

With me, he was loving, funny, provoking. Pushing. Caring. And still aloof, still not quite feeling safe with me with his secrets. I'd like to say he should have known better, but I was all of four years younger than him and so, so many years younger than him soul-wise. He was born an old soul.

I just wish I had more time with him. Especially now that I'm older and have more life behind me. Now, I think we could approach each other as almost equals (for he will always be ahead of me). Now, I can appreciate him as I could not as a teenager. Now, the pain of his loss is greater than it was as I feel his presence is so needed, and that pain grows greater still with each passing year.

I don't know how to end this book. But after reading his books, I leave you with this.

Be kind. Be respectful. Watch your words. Watch your actions. Do not take tomorrow for granted. Be who you are, but be the best of who you are, as much as you can. And when you fall, get up and brush yourself off. Forgive yourself. Admit your mistakes and move on. Give yourself grace. Take what you can from those who teach you, thank them for their knowledge, and forge your own path, for you will be the stronger for it.

Help those who have less than you do, whether it be materially or spiritually. Give when you can. Accept help as it is given to you. Ask for help when you need it.

Firm up your boundaries. Tell people what your boundaries are, as appropriate, and let them know the consequences of crossing your boundaries; then stand firm on those boundaries and those consequences. Learn when to say "no" for your mental health. Likewise, learn when to say "yes" to push you along on your journey.

Stand shoulder to shoulder, hip to hip, calf to wheel, and fight with others for what you know is right. Fight against the ills of the world.

You know what they are. Lift up those around you; create community, not divisiveness. Vote.

Find your courage to live openly and honestly about who you are and what matters to you. Find the courage to share your light.

Know you are worthy. Know you are loved. The Universe is vast and wants you to succeed in all your endeavors.

I believe that in our writing, our best selves come out. That is why in Scott's books, there was a man I was not acquainted with—because it was his best self, put on paper for all to read. And oh, how lucky we are to have his words.

Go. Be your best self. Journal. Especially in these tumultuous times, journal! I have boxes of my grandparents' journals, of my parents' journals. And I have Scott's books. I have their words to sustain me when I am alone.

What are you going to leave behind for those you love?

Thank you for reading.

Bright blessings to you and all you care about. Be well.

—Christine Cunningham Ashworth
Los Angeles, California
September 2022

APPENDIX I

Scott Cunningham: A Bibliography

A Formula Book of Magical Incenses and Oils. Self-published, 1982.

Magical Herbalism: The Secret Craft of the Wise. Minnesota: Llewellyn Publications, 1982.

Earth Power. Minnesota: Llewellyn Publications, 1983.

Cunningham's Encyclopedia of Magical Herbs. Minnesota: Llewellyn Publications, 1985.

The Magic of Incense, Oils, and Brews: A Guide to Their Preparation and Use. Minnesota: Llewellyn Publications, 1986.

The Magical Household with David Harrington. Minnesota: Llewellyn Publications, 1987.

Herb Magic (VHS Video). Minnesota: Llewellyn Publications, 1987.

The Truth about Witchcraft. Minnesota: Llewellyn Publications, 1987.

Cunningham's Encyclopedia of Crystal, Gem & Metal Magic. Minnesota: Llewellyn Publications, 1988.

The Truth about Witchcraft Today. Minnesota: Llewellyn Publications, 1988.

Wicca: A Guide for the Solitary Practitioner. Minnesota: Llewellyn Publications, 1988.

The Complete Book of Incense, Oils, and Brews. Minnesota: Llewellyn Publications, 1989. (Revised and expanded edition of *The Magic of Incense, Oils, and Brews*, 1986.)

Magical Aromatherapy. Minnesota: Llewellyn Publications, 1989.

The Magic in Food. Minnesota: Llewellyn Publications, 1990.

Earth, Air, Fire & Water. Minnesota: Llewellyn Publications, 1991.

Sacred Sleep: Dreams & the Divine. California: Crossing Press, 1992.

The Art of Divination. California: Crossing Press, 1993.

Living Wicca. Minnesota: Llewellyn Publications, 1993.

Spell Crafts with David Harrington. Minnesota: Llewellyn Publications, 1993.

The Truth about Herb Magic. Minnesota: Llewellyn Publications, 1994.

Hawaiian Religion and Magic. Minnesota: Llewellyn Publications, 1994.

The Magic of Food, Minnesota: Llewellyn Publications, 1996. (Revised edition of *The Magic in Food,* 1990.)

Pocket Guide to Fortune Telling. California: Crossing Press, 1997. (Originally published as *The Art of Divination,* 1993.)

Dreaming the Divine: Techniques for Sacred Sleep. Minnesota: Llewellyn Publications, 1999. (Revised edition of *Sacred Sleep,* 1992.)

Hawaiian Magic & Spirituality. Minnesota: Llewellyn Publications, 2000. (Revised edition of *Hawaiian Religion and Magic,* 1994.)

Cunningham's Encyclopedia of Wicca in the Kitchen. Minnesota: Llewellyn Publications, 2003. (Revised edition of *The Magic of Food,* 1996.)

Divination for Beginners: Reading the Past, Present & Future. Minnesota: Llewellyn Publications, 2003. (Formerly titled *The Art of Divination,* published by Crossing Press, 1993. Reissued by Crossing Press as *Pocket Guide to Fortune Telling,* 1997.)

Cunningham's Book of Shadows: The Path of an American Traditionalist. Minnesota: Llewellyn Publications, 2009.

Cunningham's Guide to Hawaiian Magic & Spirituality. 2009. (Third edition of *Hawaiian Magic & Spirituality,* 2000.)

Scott Cunningham's Herb Magic DVD. Minnesota: Llewellyn Publications, 2010. (DVD edition of the VHS of 1987)

Cunningham's Magical Sampler. Minnesota: Llewellyn Publications, 2012.

Dreaming the Divine: Techniques for Sacred Sleep. Minnesota: Llewellyn Publications, 2016. Second edition.

The Truth about Witchcraft. Minnesota: Llewellyn Publications, 2016. (Originally published in 1988 as *The Truth about Witchcraft Today.*)

Christine's Notes: In reading the above, I realize Scott had learned Dad's secret to writing quickly. This list doesn't include all the articles he wrote over the years for various publications. And though he was quite ill the last three years of his life, I know he wrote during that time; between 1991 and his death in March of 1993, Scott had five books published, wrote two more which were published after his death, and revised another, also published after his death.

Additionally, Scott's legacy encompasses far more than simply the English language. His works have been translated into several other languages and enjoyed worldwide. Here are his Spanish titles:

La Verdad Sobre la Brujería Americana. Minnesota: Llewellyn Español, 1998.

La Verdad Sobre la Magia de las Hierbas. Minnesota: Llewellyn Español, 1998.

Enciclopedia de cristales, gemas y metales mágicas. Minnesota: Llewellyn Español, 1999.

Enciclopedia de las hierbas mágicas. Minnesota: Llewellyn Español, 1999.

Inciensos, Aceites, e Infusiones: Recetario mágico. Minnesota: Llewellyn Español, 1999.

La casa mágica: Fortalezca su hogar con amor, salud y felicidad. Minnesota: Llewellyn Español, 2000.

Poderes terrenales: Técnicas para la magia natural. Minnesota: Llewellyn Español, 2000.

Que es la Wicca? Brujeria de hoy. Minnesota: Llewellyn Español, 2001.

Suenos Divinos: Interprete los mensajes de los dioses. Minnesota: Llewellyn Español, 2001.

Herbalismo mágico. Minnesota: Llewellyn Español, 2003.

Magia terrenal: El arte de trabajar con las fuerzas de la naturaleza. Minnesota: Llewellyn Español, 2003.

Wicca: Una guía para la práctica individual. Minnesota: Llewellyn Español, 2003.

APPENDIX II

Contributor Biographies

Mat Auryn is a witch, professional psychic, and occult teacher. He is the multi-award-winning author of the international best-selling books *Psychic Witch* and *Mastering Magick*. He is a High Priest in the Sacred Fires Tradition of Witchcraft. Mat has had the honor and privilege of studying under some of the most prominent witchcraft teachers, elders, and witchcraft traditions. He is blog manager at *Modern Witch*, has a column in *Witches and Pagans* magazine entitled "Extra-Sensory Witchcraft," and has been featured in various magazines, radio shows, podcasts, books, anthologies, and other periodicals. Find Mat at *www.matauryn.com*.

Stephanie Rose Bird is a practicing Green Witch and Hoodoo. She is a magick maker with a passion for African diasporic spirituality, folklore, and mythology. Stephanie writes a column for *Witches and Pagans* magazine. She is the author of seven books, including *Sticks, Stones, Roots and Bones, The Healing Power of African American Spirituality, African American Magick,* and *365 Days of Hoodoo: Daily Rootwork, Mojo and Conjuration.* Stephanie contributed to *The Llewellyn Complete Book of North American Folk Magic.* She is an avid swimmer, artist, herbalist, aromatherapist, mom, wife, and animal companion. Visit Stephanie at *www.stephanierosebird.com.*

Amy Blackthorn is the award-winning author of several best-selling books aimed at connecting readers with botanical spirits. She has been described as an "arcane horticulturalist" for her lifelong work with magical herbalism. Amy's work led her to start a magical tea shop called Blackthorn's Botanicals to help bridge the gap between our daily rituals and the magick we seek in our daily lives. She has appeared on HuffPoLive, Netflix's *Top Ten Secrets and Mysteries*, and the AP Newswire. Amy lives in Delaware. Find her at *amyblackthorn.com*.

Ethony Dawn is the author of *Your Tarot Court* and is a tarot and oracle deck creator, headmistress of the Tarot Readers Academy, and High Priestess of the Awakened Soul Coven. Learn more about Ethony at *ethony.com*.

James Divine is a palm reader, a mystic, and a joy monger. He has been studying palmistry for over thirty-five years and is the creator of the Divine Hand method of palmistry. James is also High Priest of Spectrum Grove in Seattle, having practiced in the Sylvan Tradition of witchcraft since 1998. James teaches palmistry in an apprenticeship program, presents workshops across the country on various esoteric and magical topics, and is currently working on his first book. James lives in Seattle with his husband and is a proud stepdad and grandpa. Find James at *thedivinehand.com*.

Jaymi Elford uses tarot to explore the world we live in and create meaning. She wrote the award-nominated *Tarot Inspired Life* and designed the *Triple Goddess Tarot*. Jaymi can be found at *www.shadesofmaybe.com*.

Amie Emberharte is an eclectic practitioner, incorporating tarot, life coaching, music, numerology, vocal coaching, spell casting, and mediumship for over three decades of professional practice. Amie provides services to a global clientele, writes a regular column for *The Carto-mancer Magazine*, and is a popular presenter at holistic and metaphysical conferences. Find Amie at *emberharte.com.*

Storm Faerywolf is a professional author, experienced teacher, visionary poet, and practicing warlock. He was trained in various streams of witchcraft, most notably the Faery tradition, where he holds the Black Wand of a Master. He is chancellor of Modern Witch University, a co-founder of Black Rose, an online course in modern folkloric witchcraft, a columnist for *The Wild Hunt,* and is host of the Witch Power Daily podcast. He has written several books including *The Stars Within the Earth, Betwixt & Between, The Witches' Name,* and *The Satyr's Kiss.* For more, visit *www.faerywolf.com.*

Beverly Frable offers classes and presentations that dive deep into divination-related topics that enhance a reader's perspectives. Visit her Facebook page, Tarot Connections, or follow her on Instagram @Beverly_Tarot_Connections.

Nancy Hendrickson is the author of numerous books including *Ancestral Grimoire* and *Ancestral Tarot,* a guidebook for communicating with your ancestors of blood, time, and place. She can be found on Instagram @nancysageshadow or on her website *www.sageandshadow.com.*

Dorothy Morrison is the owner of Wicked Witch Studios, which produces magical candles, room sprays, and oils. She's also the author of *Utterly Wicked: Hexes, Curses, and Other Unsavory Notions* and many other books. Find Dorothy at *www.wickedwitchstudios.com.*

Nicholas Pearson has been involved in all aspects of the mineral kingdom for nearly thirty years. He is among the foremost experts on crystals, combining his background in mineral science with his love of healing, spirituality, and folklore to illustrate how and why crystals can change our lives. The award-winning author of eight books including *Crystal Basics* and *Stones of the Goddess*, Nicholas lives in Orlando, Florida, with his husband. Visit him at *www.theluminouspearl.com* or on Facebook, Instagram, and @theluminouspearl.

Lynne Redd is retired and enjoys life to its fullest.

Michelle Welch is the author of *The Magic of Connection, Spirits Unveiled,* and *Pendulum Palooza,* with two more books and a crystal deck out soon. She is the owner of three SoulTopia Holistic Boutiques in Dallas, Texas. As an attorney and former trial advocacy adjunct professor, she has lent her intuitive abilities to numerous court cases. She is the host of the SoulWhat podcast and the SoulTopia YouTube channel with guests ranging from Hakeem Oluseyi to Matthew McConaughey. She is the owner of The International Divination Event in Dallas, and the Northwest Tarot Symposium in Portland, Oregon. Find her at *michellewelch.com.*

Benebell Wen is a lawyer, and the author of *Holistic Tarot* and *The Tao of Craft.* She is also the creator and illustrator of the independently produced *Spirit Keeper's Tarot* deck. Benebell can be found at *benebellwen.com.*

ABOUT THE AUTHOR

Christine Cunningham Ashworth's true love is the written word. Her writing continues the legacy left by her father, novelist Chet Cunningham and her brother Scott Cunningham, an icon of metaphysical publishing. She believes magick is everywhere and available to everyone—from tending to the garden and land spirits to utilizing breath as a tool for mindfulness, Christine lives her craft. An initiated member of The Awakened Soul Coven, she is a dedicant to Brigid and is mostly a solitary witch. She sees tarot as a storytelling medium that opens your mind to different perspectives and levels of awareness. Time spent fireside or walking along the ocean shore reinforces her heart-centeredness and speaks to her of the dynamic synchronicity of the world.

Christine is a popular speaker at writers' conferences, as well as at cartomancy conferences, such as The International Divination Event, the Northwest Tarot Symposium, and StaarCon. Christine also presents at Pagan festivals like Phoenix Phyre and Trees of Autumn Gathering. Christine's first novel came out in 2011. Since then, she has published over ten novels, numerous short stories, and the nonfiction essay collection *Wear the Pearls and Other Bits of Wisdom*. Since 2018, she has written a regular column in the *Cartomancer Magazine*. A native of San Diego, Christine lives with her husband Tom in southern California. Find out more about her at *Christine-Ashworth.com* or *mysticalmagic .me,* and @ashworthchristine on Instagram.